BETWEEN
LIVING
AND DYING

BETWEEN LIVING AND DYING

Reflections from the Edge of Experience

RUTH SCOTT

BIRLINN

First published in 2019 by
Birlinn Limited
West Newington House
10 Newington Road
Edinburgh
EH9 1QS

www.birlinn.co.uk

ISBN: 978 1 78027 616 8

British Library Cataloguing-in-Publication Data
A catalogue record for this book is available from the British Library.

Typeset by Biblichor Ltd, Edinburgh
Printed and bound by Gutenberg Press, Malta

For Mairéad
with gratitude beyond words

Contents

Acknowledgements

I owe my heartfelt thanks to a number of the teams at Southampton General Hospital, but particularly the lymphoma team under the leadership of Prof. Peter Johnson, Prof. Andy Davies and Dr Rob Lown. They, their registrars, junior doctors and specialist nurses have cared for me throughout the whole process of writing this book. They may not share the views expressed in these pages but their expertise and compassion enabled me to progress through treatment in the best possible state of mind and body and, as a result, to write about the experience and the reflections it provoked. Much of the book was written while I was an inpatient on D3, the Oncology ward. I was there for many months and felt utterly safe in the care of the nurses, health-care assistants, cleaners and caterers who became like family. Thanks, too, to Dr Andrew Jenks, who has kept me sufficiently pain-free to keep writing when the going got tough.

Mairéad, my specialist nurse, has been my constant guide. She has pulled me through. Without the trust I felt in her, I would not have had the energy to start writing in the first place. No one could have done more than she has.

My beloved Chris has been my strength and stay. Freya and Tian have continually inspired me. My wonderful friends have produced the images, poems, books, and constant affirmations of love that have given shape to this book. I'm especially grateful to Richard and Alison who provided words of comfort in the dark watches, and to Richard for believing I was writing a publishable book. Thank you for having faith in me and opening doors.

I'm grateful to Sue for correcting the grammar and punctuation of the first draft, and making helpful suggestions.

Thank you to Ann Crawford and all the team at Birlinn, especially for going above and beyond the call of duty when illness meant I could not fulfil all my responsibilities in seeking permissions. Your patience and kindness has meant a great deal.

Lastly, I thank all those women, alive and dead, named and unnamed, whose cancer treatment coincided with my own. Thank you for your song lines. They gave me strength and courage.

Foreword

When apprentice radio presenters are nervously trying to learn the craft of broadcasting, they will sometimes be counselled by veteran producers about how to do it. They are told there are two lessons they have to learn. The first is, get out of your own way, forget yourself, don't watch yourself doing this. And next, talk to the *ear* not to the *audience*. You are not addressing a multitude. You are speaking to an individual. It's all between you and another human being. Good radio broadcasters know how to keep it close and personal.

While some of this can be learned, I suspect that the best broadcasters have an instinct for it. It's what has been described as 'an original endowment of the self'. A gift. In Greek, a *charism*. That was certainly how it was with Ruth Scott during the twenty-three years she did Pause for Thought on BBC Radio 2, first with Terry Wogan, then with Chris Evans when he took over. Ruth was a charismatic broadcaster. Listeners felt she was beside them, speaking from heart to heart. And it wasn't a trick she had learned; a practised intimacy; an act. It was who she was. Ruth had the gift of *presence*, of being there for others.

A magnificent example of this was her final broadcast, when Chris Evans interviewed her in Southampton General Hospital only weeks before her death. It was no surprise that a podcast of the interview went viral. It was a not-quite-last gift to the countless people who had been nourished by her wisdom over the years. She spoke calmly of what it felt like to know that death was on its way to take her from a life that had been filled with love and achievement; a life she was sorry to leave so early; a life she was grateful for having lived.

It was characteristic of her that, not content to die well, enfolded in the love of family and friends, she wanted to observe and interrogate her own dying to find out what it might teach her and others. That's why she told Chris that during the first year of her chemotherapy she decided to write about her experiences. And this beautiful book – her last gift to us – is the result.

This is how she described what she was doing: 'As I write this book, I'm receiving intensive chemotherapy for a rare and aggressive cancer, an enteropathy-associated T-cell lymphoma, and, further down the line, the plan is for a stem cell transplant. The aim is cure, but it's not guaranteed. If all goes according to plan, it will be a year between the start of my illness and the time I may be well enough to return to work: a gap year in the shadow of death'. Sadly, there was to be no cure, no return to work. Ruth died on 20 February 2019.

Ruth was many things in her life: loving wife and mother, friend, priest, athlete, broadcaster, conflict resolver, writer. But above all, she was a nurturer, a healer. She had come to London aged eighteen to train as a nurse, and that background shows in the professional attention she brought to the treatment she received in hospital, as well as in her warmth towards the doctors and nurses who ministered to her. That's why this book is not for the faint-hearted. In these pages you will read vivid descriptions of her treatment and its consequences – and the humour that often attended both. It is a wrenching read, but it is also funny and affectionate. And it is a magnificent tribute to Britain's National Health Service and the people who make it work, often against incredible odds.

But it is much more than that. That's because Ruth Scott was a teacher as well as a healer. And she wanted to learn from what was happening to her. She said she wanted her book to be 'a meditation on life, not death, offering observations and asking questions that have occurred to me through this gap year'.

The first lesson she learned was personal: to let go of control. Then the philosopher kicked in, and she began to wonder if her cancer wasn't a metaphor for what is happening in the human community today. She informs us that cancer cells are 'ordinary cells that go into division overdrive, producing more and more of themselves, becoming distorted in the process and destructive to the body to which they belong'. A perfect metaphor for the human condition. It was this tragic divisiveness in the world that had prompted Ruth to become a mediator and facilitator in the field of conflict resolution, a role that took her into many dangerous and violent places.

The mediator is at work in this book too. She advises us in situations of conflict to articulate our concerns and grievances. Well, most of us are good at that. We fill the land with our noisy protestations. Much more difficult is listening to the other side. Here she invites us to prepare arguments 'supporting the view with which we most strongly disagree'. Reading that challenged me to interrogate my own compulsions. When I hear someone expounding a point of view with which I vehemently disagree, I am rarely listening: I am preparing my counter-blast, ramming shells into my biggest guns. Thank you, Ruth, for disarming me.

But there's more. She tells us that what most people find difficult is not change as such, but loss. Another gift. This book is full of them. Sip it slowly.

As well as her own wise teaching, another richness of this book is the wealth of quotations from poets and other writers Ruth uses to illuminate her reflections. One of them is from Michael Ondaatje's *The English Patient*:

> We die containing a richness of lovers and tribes, tastes we have swallowed, bodies we have plunged into and swum up as if rivers of wisdom, characters we have climbed into as if trees, fears we have hidden in as if caves. I wish for all this to be marked on my body when I am dead. I believe in such cartography . . .

Ruth Scott is gone, but she has left us a map to guide us through our own lives.

Richard Holloway
July 2019
Edinburgh

Introduction

Apart from a short lull in the early morning, there are always ambulances coming and going beneath my window. All life is there: babies barely visible under the plethora of intensive care tubes and monitors; elderly men and women swathed in blankets; anxious relatives trailing behind the trolleys. The walking wounded of all ages and, of course, those made stupid with drink shouting out their fury against the ambulance personnel seeking to help them and the police called in to constrain them. All have been brought here for treatment that will diagnose, cure or contain their illnesses and injuries, or take them down the road to end-of-life care. A few days ago I was one of them, transferred from the emergency treatment I needed in my local casualty department to the Oncology ward in the teaching hospital where I've been receiving ongoing care.

As I write this book I'm receiving intensive chemotherapy for a rare and aggressive cancer, an enteropathy-associated T-cell lymphoma, and, further down the line, the plan is for a stem cell transplant. The aim is cure, but it's not guaranteed. If all goes according to plan, it will be a year between the start of my illness and the time

I may be well enough to return to work: a gap year in the shadow of death.

In the middle of the night, when the ambulances' reversing alarms shatter the silence, it is not death which preoccupies my mind but life, and what I do or don't make of it. Have I been awake or sleepwalking through it, thoughtlessly going through the motions, or relentlessly impelled on by internal drives I think I understand but never quite manage to harness more creatively? The valley of the shadow of death is a thought-provoking place in which to consider human experience, my own and others'. Sitting by my window overlooking the ambulances while my chemotherapy drugs drip through the intravenous line, I have time to reflect on what has been, what is and, should I live to tell the tale, what might be. So-called normal life looks very different from the perspective of this vale.

I wonder at times if my cancer is a metaphor for what's happening in our present culture: put simply, cancer cells are ordinary cells that go into division overdrive, reproducing more and more of themselves, becoming distorted in the process and destructive to the body to which they belong. It seems my immune responses have lost their capacity to recognise and deal with cancer cells. This micro-dynamic appears replicated in relation to how we function on a wider scale. All around me I see people whose lives are distorted by profound stress as they struggle to address the destructive fallout of a pace of life over which they feel they have little control. It's not a new phenomenon. In every age there are those who fall by the wayside in the struggle to survive. What is unique to our present experience is the speed and impact of scientific and technical change. Even positive developments require periods of adjustment. We have access to more information than we can process, and the lack of time and opportunity for careful reflection as we rush headlong into the future stirs up a whirlwind of conditions and consequences that are creating divisive conflict, as well as unjust and unsustainable expectations of humankind and the earth which has nurtured us thus far.

That's why this book is a meditation on life, not death, offering observations and asking questions that have occurred to me through this gap year away from the 'everyday', and sharing the insights of those who have inspired me along the way. Right from the start of this journey I decided to read any books, essays, papers, poems or quotations that friends gave or recommended to me. I have included some but not all of the poems that have been meaningful to me through this time. At the end of the book, I have added notes on three poems that touched me but could not be included. It was a delight to find, so often, that the poetry and prose that came my way during treatment was relevant to chapters I was writing at the time.

This is not a systematic, academic treatise, although I hope it is intelligent in expression. Life is messy and complicated and I have never found my thinking neatly ordered. In this book I explore different aspects of human experience that have arisen during treatment. In that process I have become aware of an overarching theme of separation, the disconnection we experience within ourselves, from others and from the wider environment. As I've gone along I've raised questions about what we accept as normal life and wondered about the need to do things differently.

When I was first diagnosed, as a means of feeling I had some control in the situation, I was keen to see treatment as a pilgrimage, something from which I would learn much. The first lesson, as it turned out, was an essential learning to let go of control, of not having to make something good out of something bad, of not trying to grasp the reins steering this crazy horse of cancer. Unexpectedly

I had an 'Ah yes!' moment when my friend, Melanie, sent me a verse from St Paul's letter to the Romans. I am not a fan of people quoting scripture at me. Too often such quotes are taken wildly out of context and have been used more as bullets to destroy perceived heresy, rather than to build bridges of understanding, but that's not Melanie, and her choice of verse was spot on:

> Likewise the Spirit helps us in our weakness; for we do not know how to pray as we ought; but that very Spirit intercedes with sighs too deep for words.[1]

I felt in those words my degree of unwellness was recognised, as was the depth of its impact upon me. Most importantly, they left me feeling speech wasn't necessary and I hadn't got to resolve it all, but simply live through it. Others would hold it for me. It was a call to stop trying, to simply 'be', and to not feel so responsible. This is hard to articulate because it was not about being irresponsible, or not playing my part. It was more about relinquishing the sense of being driven and the toll that it has taken on who I am. What a relief! In the early weeks after the diagnosis I was able to let go of the pressure I've always placed upon myself, consciously or unconsciously, to achieve. Paradoxically, the thoughts that gradually began to emerge as I gave up on the need to 'make something of all this' came unforced into my mind and naturally began to form themselves into the words you're now reading. At that point, whether or not they became a book wasn't my priority. It was just a helpful way to pass the time in my hospital side-room when I had the capacity to concentrate. For this reason I had no structure in mind when I started writing, and much of it is written in the present tense.

I became ill at Christmas 2016, wrote most of this book during my hospital admissions in 2017, added the epilogue after complications arising in 2018, and completed editing just before Christmas 2018. The first draft ended up in a mix of present and past tenses, depending on whether I was writing up what was happening at the time or reflecting back on it. This was sometimes confusing for my initial readers. In response, apart from in this introduction, I have put most of my hospital narrative into the past tense. While the book begins and ends with the personal experiences that began and ended the time covered by the book, other illustrations from my treatment with which I open the intervening chapters are not always in chronological order. This is because, in the editing, it made more sense to make the order of themes explored the priority.

In the same way that cancer enabled me to relinquish the pressure I placed on myself to achieve, it also released me from what might be considered more overtly religious responses to my situation. I became ill not long after we moved to a new home in a new place, so I was not familiar with the priests and people at the cathedral, nor the lovely folk at the Quaker meeting I started attending. All were immensely generous in their offering of support, but I knew the people I wanted around me at this time were family, close friends and the lymphoma team. Formal church liturgies in their length and wordiness became an irrelevant endurance test I was unwilling to undergo.

To make the cancer diagnosis it was necessary to operate on my small intestine to gain biopsies of the lymphoma tissue. While recovering from this surgery I discovered the hospital chapel. It was a wonderful place to sit contemplatively alone by its water feature and greenery. I attended one Sunday service but didn't want to repeat that experience because it felt meaningless. The Baptist chaplain came by, early on in my long hospital stays. I enjoyed seeing him and was moved that when he offered to pray at the end of his first visit and I declined, saying I felt more comfortable with silence, he was willing to be silent with me. I felt no need for overt religious practice. I guess that was part of the letting-go and seeing what, if anything, emerged. I wasn't interested in the platitudes and simplistic understanding of suffering that some people of faith offered me.

I was grateful for all the people, known and unknown to me, that I knew were praying for me, and uplifted by the positive energy I think prayer creates, but I cannot accept an image of a God who heals me because people pray for that, while leaving millions of others to suffer. When someone offers to pray for me I want to know what they think they are doing.

Living with cancer makes me understand more of 'prayer' as the spontaneous utterances, inspirations and moments of awareness that well up within us and between us, and give shape to our deepest being. Prayer may arise in anguished or ecstatic souls, and often looks nothing like the formulaic recitations that tend to bear its name. I know many friends who find comfort and strength in the daily discipline of saying Morning and Evening Prayer, but it is not how I choose to pray. There are so many words, many of the sentiments of which I have ceased to believe. For the most part I have come to see prayer primarily as lived experience, not set words. Carol Ann Duffy captures this beautifully in her poem 'Prayer':

> Some days, although we cannot pray, a prayer
> utters itself. So, a woman will lift
> her head from the sieve of her hands and stare
> at the minims sung by a tree, a sudden gift.
>
> Some nights, although we are faithless, the truth
> enters our hearts, that small familiar pain;
> then a man will stand stock-still, hearing his youth
> in the distant Latin chanting of a train.

Pray for us now. Grade 1 piano scales
console the lodger looking out across
a Midlands town. Then dusk, and someone calls
a child's name as though they name their loss.

Darkness outside. Inside, the radio's prayer –
Rockall. Malin. Dogger. Finisterre.[2]

Ah, the shipping forecast! Who would have seen that as a mantra? Yet to my friend Paulie, who had loved listening to the shipping forecast for as long as he could remember, it was a source of comfort as he lay dying of an inoperable cancer.

From Scotland, my dear friend Alison sent me the photo of a tile with fishing boats and their home ports named upon it and, as I savoured the names of the boats in my hospital bed, I was transported to harbours and high seas and a sense of wildness and strength and freedom. The boats were:

> *The Rose* of Appledore
> *The Welcome* of Freckleton
> *The Flying Foam* of Bridgwater
> *The Gleaner* of Runcorn
> *The First Fruits* of Bridport

Another friend, Rachel, always brought images of the Isle of Iona, one of my favourite settings, so I could take myself there for a while in my imagination, and feel the healing power of that place. Other friends sent photos of beautiful objects, places or paintings. They were surprise gifts bringing light into the darker times when the side-effects of treatment were tough. That's why letting go of control and how I live normally has been so important for me, because wisdom often turns out to be where I don't expect it, prayer emerges when I don't try to make it, and life reveals so much more when I don't think I've got it all sewn up, particularly, it seems, in the valley of the shadow of death.

1

Living with uncertainty

In Greek mythology the River Styx is the boundary between the living world and the land of the dead, Hades. Few people cross it and return. None of those who do come back are unchanged by what is often a bruising experience. In all the great myths of the major world faith traditions, rivers, like mountains, deserts and seas, are liminal spaces marking the change from one way of being to another, sometimes with the reality of personal mortality needing to be faced so that it is no longer feared.

In the months after my diagnosis, I did not literally go into the land of the dead, just the valley of the shadow of death, though many of the new friends with cancer with whom I shared the journey died: Mary, Rosie, Ann, Grace, Sylvia, Sonya, Carol . . . the list of women who touched me with their quiet courage and unobtrusive kindness and compassion goes on. We sat quietly with one another through nights when the pain was crippling, acted as gofers when one or other of us was less mobile, provided shoulders to cry on and provoked laughter in one another at the undignified moments, moments when enemas were more explosive than expected, or the shower room became an assault course of all our bedpans of wee waiting to be measured and tested by staff rushed off their feet and too stretched to collect them.

My own personal version of the Styx is a corridor in my local hospital. On one side is the doctors' consulting room, and on the other, the dayroom of the Medical Assessment ward. It was in the doctors' room one afternoon at the end of March 2017 that a young house doctor told me that the CT scan I'd had a couple of hours earlier showed changes in my small intestine consistent with lymphoma. It was the first time that concrete evidence existed for the diagnosis I had suspected for some months. I was strangely relieved.

The doctor wanted to move swiftly to get biopsies, and so she asked if I would stay to be admitted to the Medical Assessment ward. As an inpatient, there was a higher chance that I could get on to the endoscopy list for the next day, and have biopsies taken. It meant sitting in the corridor for a couple of hours until a bed became available. No problem, I said. Chris, my husband, stayed for an hour, but, eventually, I suggested that he went home. I was fine, and there was no point in two of us waiting. I became less fine as two hours turned to four, then six, then eight. A draughty corridor was not the place to sit alone as the reality of a life-threatening diagnosis sank in, but, finally, nine hours later, I made it into the ward dayroom, and an hour after that, at midnight, a bed was ready for me.

That corridor marked the transition for me between normal life and the valley of the shadow of death. Some people describe the change between the time when everything in their lives is fine and the sudden experience of trauma or tragedy as taking them into a parallel universe where nothing is familiar. In the early days of being in this unfamiliar territory, an image used by Teilhard de Chardin, the French philosopher and Jesuit priest, captured for me this profound sense of dislocation. He wrote of those moments when we 'lose all foothold within ourselves'.[1] For him this is a state to be actively sought so that we become the space into which God may come but, in my experience, deep trauma may also impose upon us this loss of self. Since it is unlooked-for, there is no guarantee that anything we might describe as divine will infuse the emptiness. A friend whose son was killed in a tragic accident identified profoundly with a dead fox she found one day by the side of the road, snuffed out in an instant by a passing car. Like the fox, with the cars hurtling past its lifeless body, she felt dead inside while life continued as usual around her. She was no longer part of it. Human existence looks different for people who suddenly find themselves confronted by their own mortality or that of the people they love. It's not that this isn't life just as much as so-called normal life may be, but it is qualitatively different.

Later in my treatment, my friend Marion sent me two postcards, both self-portraits by Rembrandt. One was a sketchy black and white etching; the other a full-blown oil painting. Marion thought the sketchy image was like my life in the shadow of death and the oil painting was like my normal life. I wasn't so sure. It's true that, with life-threatening illness, the illusion of security with which many of us live disappears and existence suddenly appears very fragile and 'sketchy'. But, although living with cancer seemingly narrowed my life considerably, it also brought an unexpected rich-ness and depth of insight. My priorities changed. I came to see things differently and was glad of the experience.

During a rare few days out of hospital in the middle of treat-ment, I sat in the Quaker Meeting for Worship where I'm a member and became completely absorbed in the windows. I was struck by how, where the sunlight hit the glass, they were impossible to see through because of the smearing being illuminated – but where the wisteria leaves cast their shadow on the panes I could see clearly through the glass. The image seemed to connect with my experience: in the shadow of death, vision becomes clearer. The abnormalities of normal life are thrown into sharp relief. The extraordinary landscape of life-threatening human experiences – in my case, this rare and aggressive cancer requiring surgery, intensive chemotherapy and stem cell transplant – became the ordinary everyday for the duration, while to those looking on from normal life it remained shocking and difficult to accept.

The hard part was moving *between* normal life and the valley of shadow. I noticed that on the days when I was in good shape for the state I was in, perhaps having enjoyed an ordinary activity like walking into town and feeling very much in the land of the living, I was utterly thrown by catching sight of my bald head and the permanent IV line in my arm reflected in a shop window. I needed those occasional days of normal life, but they were unsettling as well when the reality of being seriously ill intruded into them. I'll say more about this later in the chapter.

A number of friends said how unfair it was that I had cancer, but I've never felt that. Life happens. We are the product of all the generations that have gone before us, the genetic inheritances, the times and places in which we live, the experiences of joy and grief we have. Why not me? I certainly don't believe in a God who would *give* me this suffering. I simply see it as life evolving in all its creative and destructive complexity as it has from the time of the Big Bang. Through treatment, my infinitesimally small part in that story concerned how I chose to respond to the unexpected development of cancer. My international working life, lived at high speed, shrank to playing my part as positively as I was able in getting me well, if that was possible. My achievements, if such they were, changed. Before my diagnosis I had worked with the casualties of violent conflict around the world in trauma care or peace-building; I had talked to millions on the radio; run retreats and workshops around the country. Now, I was rejoicing, as on one particular day after abdominal surgery, at being able simply to pass wind! Such things require a radical shift in thinking, often a change in how we understand ourselves and our worth as human beings.

When I first became ill, in December 2016, I was coughing and struggling to breathe, waking with night sweats and spiking temperatures. Chronic obstructive pulmonary disease, then pulmonary embolism and pleurisy all came up as potential diagnoses. Blood tests confirmed something wasn't right, but working out what it was took longer. In January, I looked up my symptoms on the internet. Lymphoma emerged as a possibility, but the evidence needed to confirm that diagnosis didn't come easily. A gastroscopy and colonoscopy showed nothing (because neither endoscopy could reach the bit of intestine where my cancer had produced lesions). I was thrown by the results. I should have been glad no problem was revealed, but I knew how ill I was becoming, and the spectre of childhood experience – when I'd been unwell but not believed – rattled my equilibrium. What if the doctors didn't believe me now? Reality indicated that they knew well enough that something was not right and that my fear of not being taken seriously was irrational. It's not uncommon for the vulnerability of illness to highlight the raw points in our psyches as well as plugging into our strengths.

For three months, I visited my GP surgery more times than I had done in my whole life before. I was always referred on to the local hospital. I lost a lot of weight. I carried on working while recognising that I was becoming more and more unwell. One evening, after a couple of days co-facilitating a difficult conversation for a group in London, I set off for home. As I packed the car and drove away, abdominal pain kicked in, making it hard to breathe normally. I felt really cold and couldn't get the car warm enough. The motorway I needed was closed and traffic had backed up for miles. Eventually I took a diversionary route, set the SatNav, but missed a vital turning. A two-hour journey took four hours. Ten miles from home, on a B road in the middle of goodness-knows-where, pins and needles started in my hands. I pulled off the road and began to get out of the car but that made me dizzy and I fell back inside. The pins and needles spread to my legs. I wondered if I was having a stroke. I lay there calming myself until the symptoms passed. Eventually, I was able to get out and walk around a little before setting off again. By the time I got home, I was shivering uncontrollably. My temperature was very high and I felt wretched. The next day, I woke up feeling fine and carried on. Eventually, however, the symptoms began to affect my concentration at work and the need for further investigations, including diagnostic surgery, was apparent. At the end of March, after the diagnosis, I realised I could no longer keep going as I was. Reluctantly, I cleared my diary.

It took time to discover what was wrong with me. What struck me as the illness took hold was that waiting for results, living with uncertainty, was far more crippling than receiving a confirmed diagnosis, even if the latter was of a disease that might kill me. I'm not alone in this. Many of my fellow cancer sufferers have expressed the same. It's not a perspective exclusive to those facing the possibility of serious illness. What harms people in all kinds of tragedies, or even simply in trying to get by in straitened life circumstances, is uncertainty and the waiting for information that often comes with that.

Uncertainty is not necessarily all bad. My friend, analytical psychotherapist Melanie Gibson, playfully imagines uncertainties as angels.[2] In biblical stories people wrestle with angels, sometimes unsure whether it is a human foe or holy messenger with whom they struggle. Even when they bring glad tidings, the presence of angels heralds life-changing experiences that may be as disturbing as they are joyful. I liked that image because it meant that in the context of my illness I imagined I must be surrounded by a heavenly host, such were the uncertainties!

The 'angels' that are uncertainties inhabit the emotional landscape between the known and the unknown. Their presence may be painful but there is also great potential for our understanding to be deepened and to be opened up and opened out, if we are prepared to work with these uncertainties. Uncertainty is a characteristic of any time of transition and change, something we need to help our children embrace fearlessly, rather than trying to shield them from. Developing the resilience to live with uncertainty can be tough, particularly if you have the type of personality that likes the 'i's dotted and the 't's crossed. I suspect that's why many of us prefer to accept as real the illusion that life is secure, change is to be avoided and we're in control.

Thinking about the impact of the uncertainty that I have been forced to confront has made me alert to the uncertainties others are facing in the world beyond my hospital ward. I became conscious that while uncertainties hold potential for growth, imposing unnecessary uncertainty on others should always be avoided where possible. In June of my gap year, a terrible fire in Grenfell Tower, a block of flats in London, killed seventy-one men, women and children. What distressed the survivors and those whose relatives remained on the missing list, and drove them to angry protest, was being left in a position of not knowing: not knowing the exact death toll; not knowing for sure if their loved ones had died; not knowing where they were going to live or for how long they would have to wait until they could be properly resettled; not knowing where to go for help and advice; finding that those in positions of responsibility for their circumstances were being less than clear, even reluctant, in giving them the information they needed, or explaining why some of what they needed to know would take time to find out. Trust was made doubly difficult because the fire was preceded by a time when the concerns of the residents had not been addressed by the council they now needed to help them in the emergency.

Grenfell was a terrible tragedy in its own right, but it is not a solitary event. In every time and place similar avoidable calamities hit individuals and communities through the lack of necessary care or resources required by human beings to live and work out healthy and fulfilled lives. With limited power and choice, it is often the more vulnerable members of a community, here as well as abroad, whose experience is thrown into chaos and grief, and who bear the brunt of man-made disasters.

Major tragedies may not strike every day, but all around us there are individuals struggling against unjust systems and patterns imposed by the inhumanity, thoughtlessness or indifference of others. My courageous niece, who lives with physical and learning challenges, wanted to reduce her four cleaning jobs to just two that gave her the same hours and pay but with less of the exhausting rushing from one place to the next. She had a half-time cleaning post with a company she loved, and was keen to take a half-time role in another company close to home. The latter wanted her, but initially demanded she work only for them, even though they would not guarantee how many hours they would give her or when she'd need to come in. Thankfully my niece had family to help her challenge this unreasonable expectation, but how many people have either the nerve or the support to achieve a more just way of working?

For employers, workers are two a penny and there's always someone desperate to take any job no matter how unjust the conditions may be. Why is it thought acceptable by some to impose practices on others that they would not dream of accepting themselves unless, of course, they had full control of when they did or didn't work? How have we become so removed from the lives of others that we either do not understand or do not care how our decisions hurt them and treat them in ways we would not want to be treated ourselves? This is not a new phenomenon. In my time it may take the form of zero-hours contracts, for example, but throughout human history those with power and choice have repeatedly played their part in the exploitation of others for personal gain.

Uncertainty drains energy, increases stress and is the last thing traumatised people need to deal with. Given how destructive it can be, it seems extraordinary to me that we leave people in such states when we could operate much more humane systems. I suspect that it's not until we find ourselves directly affected by similar tragedy that we realise just how debilitating and unjust are many official responses to tragedy.

I've been aware for years how disabled men and women have struggled with people and processes that consistently fail them. Attempts to lead independent lives are thwarted by environments that limit or prevent mobility and accessibility. Accessing legitimate benefits is a nightmare. Yet it was only through my cancer that I began to comprehend the enormity of the barriers we put in the way of others simply seeking the same opportunities we expect for ourselves. Even something as straightforward as applying for allowances I was entitled to receive almost defeated me.

Illness meant I could no longer earn a living. Doctors told me it would be at least nine months before I might be able to work again. My much-needed full-time freelance income disappeared overnight. The first government grant I was advised to apply for turned out to be a forty-page application that completely floored me in my seriously sick state. What about others for whom lack of literacy might immediately make it an impossible hoop to leap through? Macmillan Cancer Care came to my aid by providing financial advisors who could guide me. As it turned out, because I had spent more time in hospital than at home at the time of applying, I was not eligible for the grant I'd been directed towards. I was helped to apply for other assistance. It took months to sort out before I started receiving a small amount of money. Luckily, since I have no private pension plan, I had been putting aside money to remedy that omission, so I had this resource to continue to pay bills. I felt that if I got back to working I would be able to build it up again. If I didn't survive my illness, I wouldn't need the money anyway, but what about families where the one suddenly unable to work has no reserves and the immediate need to feed the family and pay utility bills remains? Where is the compassion and empathy in all the bureaucracy that such people face when they need the money they are legitimately entitled to receive as soon as possible, without all the uncertainty about whether or not they'll get it?

As I observed wider life from the confines of my life with lymphoma, I was struck by the extent to which we live in a society where, corporately, justice and compassion are too frequently replaced by greed and indifference to the plight of others. How can some employers enjoy far more income than they need or deserve while knowing some of their workers are struggling to make ends meet, sometimes having to decide between paying for food or heating, not because they are foolish with money but simply because not enough is coming in to pay for the basic necessities? If a truly civilised society is one that cares well for its most vulnerable citizens, we are not as civilised a community as we may like to think. I do not accept that to believe we should and could operate with greater humanity is idealistic or naïve. That kind of cynicism is a get-out clause for indifferent, ignorant, exhausted or complacent people who have no desire to change a status quo that works for them. The psychological as well as physical distance that exists between one person and another often means we have no understanding of the lives others are sometimes forced to live.

As I reflected on these things in my hospital room, I found my assessments echoed in the journals of Philip Toynbee, poet, author and one-time reviewer for the *Observer*. My friend, Rowan, had suggested I read his work. While I was still growing up, Toynbee was already wrestling with the 'cruel and grasping indifference to the pain of others' that he perceived in wider society.[3] But it's only part of the picture. Precisely because I was in hospital I was also aware of other human reactions. I knew first-hand the considered actions, reflective generosity and empathetic responsiveness to the anguish others experience, and the personal examination and openness to life beyond our own perspective exhibited by many of the people caring for me. Their example echoed that of so many people I've met and worked with over the years.

Toynbee's observations of trends in the world around him caused him to reflect deeply on his personal responses and the mental guilt and distress he felt about his own shortcomings. As I read his words I was reminded how greed, cynicism and indifference exist in each of us alongside the more positive characteristics I've mentioned. I'm just as capable of turning a blind eye to another's pain and switching off the sound when charity appeals come on the TV and compassion fatigue kicks in. There's only so much I can do, so many people I can care about, and sometimes I want to shut out the rest of the world in all its many shades of humanity and inhumanity. But whether I like it or not, the world explodes into my living room and conversations. I need to note and be responsive to the negatives, but it's important to my well-being that I take time to register heart-warming human dynamics that come to the fore, even as horror threatens to destroy them.

Terrorist attacks as well as tragic accidents have brought out the best as well as the worst in human nature. Men and women who normally live quiet lives suddenly take heroic action when their lives and the lives of those around them are under threat. People who usually keep themselves to themselves feel moved to gather in community to share grief, to respond to practical needs, to be what in normal everyday life we seem to have less time or inclination to be.

I know that some of the women with whom I've shared my cancer journey would not be people among my close friendship group outside this experience of life-threatening illness. We have connected deeply because in life's critical situations there are deeper human bonds that come into play, common experiences uniting us in some powerful way. It suggests that when life is running more smoothly we live at a more superficial level with the people who are beyond our intimate relationships. Perhaps that's not surprising. In normal life deeper connectedness takes time and effort. In crisis contexts, a lot of the usual 'feeling our way' with others is bypassed by the impact of what has happened. We don't have time for the small talk or usual conventions of getting to know others (or do we prefer to keep them at bay?) Perhaps in ordinary life we could practise a little more widely the humane responses that may only see the light of day in more challenging circumstances. We so desperately need them in our local communities, and they are our responsibility as much as anyone else's.

Responding with greater compassion and understanding may require we go outside our comfort zone to listen to those whose experiences and attitudes are utterly different from our own, and that requires humility. What do I mean by humility in this context? Humility recognises that my understanding of life is like having just one piece of a jigsaw. No one stands where they stand without reason. The reasons may be due to positive or negative experiences that may be utterly different from our own. When I listen to you, I may not share your perceptions, but the fact that your life is not the same as mine opens the opportunity for me to learn more about what lies beyond my limited perspective; to add further pieces to the picture of existence I'm putting together.

One aspect of the truth I have learned over time is that not all uncertainties and situations of waiting can be quickly resolved. There may be no other option but to wait. My diagnosis could not be reached immediately. Answers may not come quickly in complex situations. For example, though families of those who died in the Grenfell Tower fire needed to know exactly how many and who died in the blaze, finding out who was in the building – whether they lived there or were visiting – took time. Those seeking the bodies in the burnt-out block had to move carefully lest the structure collapse upon them. It was heart-breaking work. It couldn't be rushed, no matter what the pressure from those who grieved or who did not know if they had a reason to grieve.

Anger is an understandable response in such situations. During my hospital admissions I was struck by a tattoo that Mike, one of the wonderful health-care assistants on the D3 ward, has on his arm. It reads, 'Anger is a gift'. I know that to be true. Anger produces energy that can accomplish change. It can motivate us to work for justice in the face of the indifference of others and keep us going through difficult circumstances, but it can also be destructive if inappropriately channelled. Anyone can feel anger, but knowing how to use it appropriately and effectively is another matter. At their height, the chemicals triggered in our bodies by anger literally cut off access to the thinking parts of our brain and may lead to primitive violent responses we later regret. When we use rage against others in ways that replicate the dehumanising treatment that triggered our anger in the first place, we do the very thing that harmed us and that we hated. It's much harder to word our grievances and concerns in ways that those they are directed at can hear and respond to positively than to rant at the people who are giving us grief. Ultimately ranting helps no one, however legitimate it may be, and at some point we need to engage in a calmer, though no less honest, conversation.

Those who walk in the shadow of death need to access a range of different responses. The survivors of the Grenfell Tower fire have needed the energy of their understandable anger to challenge the incompetence and lack of understanding among those who have the power and responsibility to help them. But in my own situation anger at how my life had been turned upside-down wouldn't have been helpful. Thankfully, I didn't feel it at all. I needed to let go of what was in the past, to concentrate on navigating well my present reality. Calm acceptance of that reality enabled me to go with the flow of treatment. Later, as treatment transformed into recovery, my need was to tap into the energy of passionate resistance to the limitations treatment imposed for a while. On the days when it would be easier to give in, the determination to just take one more step helped to keep me going and lifted my spirits. It's a delicate balance to achieve, and it will be different for every person. It takes wisdom to work out when different human responses need to be brought to the fore.

The sense of dislocation I mentioned earlier in this chapter, when I was suddenly reminded in normal circumstances of my diseased state, may offer some insight here. The truth is that ordinary everyday life and exceptional life-threatening experiences require very different languages and behaviours. The Grenfell Tower survivors needed responses that were unlikely to come from the processes and procedures of normal council practice, however well-intentioned those operating such systems were. At one level this seems obvious, but perhaps less well recognised were the different mind-sets of those directly impacted by the fire, and those who through their normal daily work were trying to respond appropriately. They were inhabiting two entirely different realities, and the inability to recognise and bridge that gap added further to the pain, anger and failings in that situation.

Helping one another to understand the very different worlds of 'normal life' and the uncertainty and pain of shadow-of-death experiences depends so much on good communication. In a world where communication technology expands at a rate most of us struggle to keep up with, communication skills at a face-to-face level seem not to have improved very much, if at all. Back in 1948, Paul Tillich, theologian and philosopher, wrote, 'The walls of distance, in time and space, have been removed by technical progress; but the walls of estrangement between heart and heart have been incredibly strengthened.'[4]

For three years I was involved in planning and facilitating shared conversations across the Church of England about human sexuality. Our purpose was not to change minds but to change the way in which Christians with deeply opposing views and experiences were present for one another, how they talked and listened so that they saw the person behind the position and could speak honestly in ways that enabled the 'other' to hear where they were coming from, even if they understood life in sharply conflicting ways. Through the conversations I was struck not only by the generosity and grace of many participants but also by the number who had never come across these techniques or been taught how to have difficult conversations around issues of significant difference. Such skills are essential. Few of us live in the more insular societies with which our grandparents were familiar. Most people of their generation did not travel far from their home community or have access to men and women from very different creeds and cultures. It's clear from rising tensions today around immigration that many of us are ill-equipped to deal with the differences that increasingly exist in our local neighbourhoods. The wonderful potential for developing greater knowledge and understanding is too frequently eclipsed by profound challenges; this is particularly true in communities already stretched by poverty and deprivation, where they feel they are being imposed upon by the decisions of people in power who seem neither to understand nor care about their concerns.

This state of affairs is far removed from the experience I had in the shadow of death where all of us – patients, medical staff, caterers and cleaners – were working together with the common purpose of healing and care. Normal life lacks this sense of shared vision and common task. We often appear to be a society of disparate groups pulling in different directions, with sometimes abysmal ignorance and lack of empathy for those who are our neighbours. Is that a 'normal' we want to promote?

Before leaving the subject of the pain of waiting and uncertainty I want to touch on the belief some have expressed that, distressing and painful as these states may be, they are crucial and potentially creative strands of human experience. Kneeling in an ancient church, one of my favourite poets, R.S. Thomas, did not want divine inspiration to come too soon.[5] If I understand him correctly, he saw meaning as something to be found in the times of waiting, not in their resolution. This is a tough lesson to learn. I would far rather have the unexpected reassurance that came one day, early in my treatment, when Chris and I were waiting in a side room of the Medical Assessment ward at my local hospital. I had been admitted as an emergency with debilitating side effects from a chemotherapy treatment. The nurses at the local hospital were lovely, but I only truly felt safe when I was in the larger teaching hospital, where the Oncology wards were expert in dealing with my particular cancer and its complications. In a state of serious unwellness I was struggling to remain calm.

For some reason, Chris and I were talking about the 'still small voice' the prophet Elijah failed to hear on Mount Sinai in the Old Testament story. I'm all for still small voices or, as a better translation of the Hebrew puts it, 'the sound of thinly sliced silence', but what I really needed to calm my anxiety in that side room where I felt strangely abandoned, was some megaphone help. About two minutes after I'd said this to Chris, a sister appeared at the door and announced loudly that I was being transferred to the teaching hospital, to the ward where most of my care now was. Chris and I burst out laughing. Megaphone help indeed! His earlier call to the lymphoma team at the bigger hospital had prompted them into action that led to my transfer. I was grateful beyond words. It was a rare and delightful example of uncertainty being resolved unexpectedly and quickly.

Yet however much I desire instant resolutions, they leave no room to develop into a deeper awareness of life and what it means to be human. In general, this illness constantly confronted me with the importance of accepting uncertainty as a sometimes unchangeable part of the journey. As such, I have already had to face loneliness, grief, the loss of what I thought I knew and the sometimes limited range of inner resources that I have to make on this journey. I would not have discovered both the absences and presences of strength and weakness within me if I'd continued racing through experience with relative ease and assurance.

As I went through intensive treatment in the early days, I knew I would have to wait two to three years before we could assess its success at curing me, unless of course, unavoidable death happened in the interim. Ahead lay a number of tough times that couldn't be bypassed but must be endured if treatment had any chance of working. Waiting and uncertainty were unavoidable parts of this process in which I was largely dependent upon the expertise of others rather than my own capacities. I was being done to, more than doing. It was a new experience for me. As I worked to make that shift in identity my friend Sue reminded me of the writing of W.H. Vanstone in his classic book *The Stature of Waiting*.[6]

Vanstone's thesis is that no matter how powerful the stories of Jesus' active ministry, his greatest and eternal impact was from the time of his arrest, his trial and crucifixion when he ceased to do and was instead done to by others. For the writers of Mark's and John's Gospels his helplessness became the point when what they saw as God's glory was truly revealed. Reflecting on the present day in the light of this thought, Vanstone argues that 'the social and economic organisation of the Western world is developing in such a way that, in ever-increasing areas and phases of life, the individual is cast in the role of patient, of recipient rather than achiever, of one who must wait and depend upon factors outside his control'.[7] At the same time, he goes on to say, people in states of helplessness, dependence, passivity and diminished ability are considered generally as being of less worth. Yet Vanstone argues that such people impact powerfully on their communities simply by 'being'. I know from my own work with men, women and children with severe learning and physical disabilities how much they contribute to life and community relations simply by their presence.

That said, the cynic in me initially saw Vanstone as an apologist wanting to make something of a frankly irredeemable situation, but putting aside theological interpretations of these accounts, at a human level, from where I now was, I realised that there is truth in his perceptions. What struck me as I read the gospel accounts of Jesus' arrest, trial and death is how his way of *being* came to the fore, as his way of *doing* receded. His dignity, his silence, his acceptance of the unavoidable, his courage, his compassion and spirit of forgiveness for others, even at the point of dying and despite his heartfelt cry of vulnerability in the words 'My God, my God, why have you forsaken me?' (Mark 15:34) move me deeply and spoke into my own experience as a patient. I was touched, too, by how many of the women I was with, facing potential death or in the last days of life, lived with quiet courage and heightened compassion. Suffering strips away superficial responses and demands we dig deeper into our hearts for the strength needed to hold steady in our precarious new position. As Joan Iten Sutherland notes, life-threatening or chronic illness brings us rapidly into confrontation with what she calls 'the Great Matter': 'We're all standing at the cliff edge of life and death all the time, it's just that, with chronic illness, you can never forget you're there.'[8]

Confronting the fragility of life, our mortality and the mortality of those dear to us, changes the way we respond in every relationship. Marian Partington, whose sister Lucy was a victim of the mass murderers Fred and Rosemary West, speaks of how 'saying goodbye to people, on a daily basis, brings with it that edge of intensity that accompanies the reality of impermanence'.[9]

Though the circumstances in which we are confronted by the essential transience of life may be traumatic, the realisation need not be frightening in the longer term, even though the way to living well with it may be painful. It puts life into perspective. In his seventy-fifth birthday lecture Professor Stephen Hawking spoke about how depression overtook him after he was diagnosed with motor neurone disease at the age of twenty-one. He went on to say, 'After my expectations had been reduced to zero, every new day became a bonus and I began to appreciate everything I did have.'[10]

For myself, I saw how my own choice to live through my time in the shadow of death – where I was done to, more than doing – with calmness, grace and gratitude, all of which I felt deeply, impacted positively not only on my well-being but also on the staff caring for me, and on those I love. Although I wanted to enable my hospital team to do all they needed to do without me complicating their work, my choice was largely selfish, the means by which I was best able to cope with what was happening to me.

But I'm skewing Vanstone's argument significantly. For Vanstone, it is not how I choose to react in the state of being done to; it is simply that in my existing in this sometimes helpless state, the world is somehow changed for the better. Perhaps the choices I have made have been the result of experiencing the many things I have done, for good or ill, but when it came to the crunch it is not my actions or attitudes that are of primary worth. It is simply that I exist. For someone who thought my identity was dependent on what I achieved in life this was an important discovery, taking me into a deeper reflection about the pace of life at which we live and the space we do or don't make room for simply 'being', rather than constantly needing to 'do'.

2

Making space

Before the hospital brought in a new catering company, the only main-course option for those of us who were on a low-residue diet was a desiccated and anaemic omelette served with pallid, pureed, reconstituted potato that looked as though it had already been through someone else's guts. The lack of palatable food at a point when I needed to regain lost weight, while avoiding any ingredients that would impact negatively on the surgery from which I was recovering, almost reduced me to tears. The possibility of dying I could deal with. It was inedible food that was my nemesis. Until that point food had always been a source of delight. It has also been something that I realise I've spent most of my life bolting down at the same speed with which I seem to do everything else. Never before have I had to eat so slowly, to chew every mouthful of tasteless pap until it could be swallowed smoothly, thus diminishing the abdominal pain that troubled me when eating.

While life-threatening illness led to emergency situations when medical action was required quickly, on the whole it radically slowed the pace of the life I was leading while 'healthy'. I use inverted commas deliberately because I wonder now just how healthy my normal life was, not because it's been particularly tough – far from it – but because far too often I've driven through, rather than been drawn into a more natural rhythm of living. If my family and friends were to be believed, I might even have lost touch with what a life-enhancing speed might be. When I became fully freelance a few years ago I felt I had a great pattern: times of intense work interspersed with periods for recovery, reflection and the exploration of new possibilities. I loved it. When I wasn't travelling, I was a breakfast regular at my local teashop, tucked in the corner with my paper, toasted tea cake and pot of vanilla black tea.

Early morning quiet times on my own were complemented by the corporate silence of the Quaker meeting on Sundays. I definitely didn't feel rushed off my feet, but somehow I left those closest to me feeling breathless because of all they saw me doing. I still haven't worked out whose perception of my working life is the more accurate, but I do know that illness slowed me right down and made me aware of supposedly normal patterns of life that may be harmful, blinding us to delights we would notice if only we weren't speeding through existence with often far too little attention to what's around us.

Sometimes these patterns are ones we impose on ourselves. Sometimes, they are imposed upon us by wider society. Either way, I wonder if we are experiencing an age that has confused quantity of life with quality of life, and values superficial speed of existence more than deeper engagement with what life could be, and what meaning we may find or create within it. What was clear as I sat in my hospital room was that there's evidence to suggest that for all the material benefits we may have, many of us are not at ease with ourselves or the world we inhabit.

Research tells me that increasing numbers of us are resorting to antidepressants to get through our days, that teenagers in the UK suffer from more stress and unhappiness than those in mainland Europe, that self-harming among adolescents is commonplace and that young men are significantly more likely than young women to take their own lives as they struggle to find their place in today's society. I've heard how, in professions like nursing or teaching, abnormally high numbers are retiring early or swapping professions, overwhelmed and frustrated by unreasonable demands and bureaucracy, and believing that there must be more to life than unending pressure.

I wonder how much this pace of life is set by folk who love to live at high speed, who have privileges of high income and leisure options that most of the population lack, and who, even more so than I am, are driven by the need to achieve, or to do better than anyone else. As our leaders work with the complexities of economics, expanding populations, immigration and greater international instability, it is perhaps easy for them to lose sight of the human cost of the decisions they make: a management mind-set is not always compatible with a human-centred ethic. That's a huge generalisation, but it contains truth.

Alongside this, technological and scientific advances are happening so quickly we're running to keep up, not always thinking through the negatives of developments even as we promote the positives. Artificial intelligence, for example, may produce all kinds of labour-saving devices, medical advances and economic advantages for businesses, but what about those who will lose their jobs as robots replace them, becoming part of the growing community of people who do not have control of their lives and who are valued less because they're not contributing in the ways 'normal' society has come to value? Do we want a society where the few benefit at the expense of the many, and living with humanity slips down the scale of our priorities? That doesn't sound like the normal I want.

A Christian Aid advert some years ago asked people to think about 'Life before Death'. Life in the present is the only time we can influence. Things don't have to be as they are, so why do we accept inhumane practices and processes? The words that come to mind in response are 'lack of empathy', 'indifference' and 'a sense of helplessness'.

Many years ago, snuggled in bed breastfeeding my baby daughter in the early morning, I was listening to a nature programme on the radio. A predator had killed a new-born seal pup and dragged it out to sea. All I could hear were the anguished cries of the mother. The impact of those cries upon me was visceral. Thirty years on those few seconds of broadcasting remain strong in my memory, like a physical imprint. I was reminded of them again as I worked my way through cancer treatment and its legacy. Stranded in my hospital bed in those moments when I was particularly unwell, I felt a profound awareness of the degree of suffering in the world, and the myriad men, women and children who never really get the chance to live before they die. As I read about their tragic existence in newspapers or watched their plight on television, my own struggles with cancer took me beyond a purely academic recognition of their pain into a physical experience of it. My heart cramped, my pulse raced, and a deep groan stirred within. How can it be that so many suffer? Like shadows passing across the sands of time, their breath barely mists the air before it is gone, and few, if any, stop to mark the moment and grieve their loss. The tragedy of it is all but overwhelming. I have been so lucky to have lived a full and rich life. I do not want others never to have had that opportunity. Somehow, however short or long my life turns out to be, and however limited my sphere of influence, I decided I must try and live and be and make space for others in such a way that, whatever burdens they carry, they are glad to be alive in the moments we meet. Somehow,

I must increase my own capacity to bear and respond more effectively to the suffering of others with which my own pain connects me.

Life-threatening illness might well have merged my humanity into the sea of human suffering, but if I was to make even a tiny contribution to stemming its flow, I must not lose sight of another key insight that came from being seriously ill and having the space to notice what previously had passed me by. The proximity of death made me all the more conscious of the preciousness of life and to see it through new eyes.

Living in the shadow of death I found my senses became all the more acute. The smell of lime blossom filled me with joy. Sounds evoked beautiful memories long forgotten. Sights could be overwhelming. After a long stint in hospital I remember returning home and sitting shell-shocked in my living room intensely aware of all the wonderful colours, the peacock blues, aquamarines and turquoises replacing the white and pale blue of my hospital setting. The greens of spring turning into summer along the roads between home and hospital had never appeared so vivid to me. The ecstasy and shock of it all is captured in the breathless, almost jumbled quality of e.e. cummings' poem, 'i thank You God', brought to my attention by my friend and colleague Gillian:

> i thank You God for most this amazing
> day: for the leaping greenly spirits of trees
> and a blue true dream of sky; and for everything
> which is natural which is infinite which is yes
>
> (i who have died am alive again today,
> and this is the sun's birthday; this is the birth
> day of life and of love and wings: and of the gay
> great happening illimitably earth)

how should tasting touching hearing seeing
breathing any – lifted from the no
of all nothing – human merely being
doubt unimaginable You?

(now the ears of my ears awake and
now the eyes of my eyes are opened)[1]

I wondered why I should be struck so deeply by what in many ways was all too familiar to me. Vanstone suggests that, 'Through our awareness of needs we become exposed to powers and qualities in the world which otherwise perhaps would pass unrecognised.'[2] In my situation, it was as though illness made me see again in the way I do when I travel abroad to new places. At such times I'm fully in the present moment, absorbing all the new sights and not wanting to miss anything. I'm not distracted by thoughts of the past or future. For how much of my life could I say that's been the case? Very little, I suspect. Instead of being fully awake in the here and now, sometimes I've sleep-walked my way through the days, agonised by past griefs, and fretting about future scenarios that rarely happen. That's as someone who knows the importance of living in the present moment! Franz Kafka's admonition in a letter to his friend, Oskar Pollak, might well have applied to me at times, 'You skewer yourself on every brief emotion for a long time, so that in the end you live for only an hour, since you have to mull for a hundred years about that hour.'[3]

In the Gospel of Luke the tension between squandering the present on needless activity and inhabiting it with complete attention is captured in the different responses of two women, Martha and Mary, when Jesus comes to visit them. Jesus is the epitome of life in all fullness, the divine presence and present. Mary recognises the moment and gives Jesus her full attention. Martha, on the other hand, is distracted by her daily tasks, and the 'oughts' and 'shoulds' she believes to be important. She resents Mary for not being driven by the same pressures and protests to Jesus. His response is clear. Martha's distractedness is not the way to live. Recognising what really matters and giving it full attention is of paramount importance. He wants her to notice the beauty of the moment, of people connecting with one another, because that's more important than rushing around being busy but blind to these precious encounters. Martha gives off the feeling of over-stretched and desiccated energy. I imagine Mary as vibrant and bright-eyed. Because she's prepared to give space to what's life-giving in her experience she's able to access new energy.

Another factor in the equation of reawakening awareness is that painful experiences accentuate moments of beauty. In the mellow hues of everyday existence things don't always stand out. When life is tough the beautiful reveals itself in sharp contrast. For a short while this beauty becomes the everything of everything. In hospital I could not read Irina Ratushinskaya's poem 'I will live and survive' without crying tears of recognition at the seemingly small but life-giving detail that caught her attention in her labour camp cell:

I will live and survive and be asked
How they slammed my head against a trestle
How I had to freeze at nights
How my hair started to turn grey
But I'll smile. And will crack some joke
And brush away the encroaching shadow
And will render homage to the dry September
That became my second birth.
And I'll be asked, 'Doesn't it hurt you to remember?'
Not being deceived by my outward flippancy
But the former names will detonate my memory –

Magnificent as old cannon.
And I will tell of the best people in all the earth,
The most tender, but also the most invincible.
How they said farewell, how they went to be tortured,
How they waited for letters from their loved ones.
And I'll be asked: what helped us to live
When there were neither letters, nor any news – only walls,
And the cold of the cell, and the blather of official lies,
And the sickening promises made in exchange for betrayal.
And I will tell you of the first beauty I saw in captivity.
A frost-covered window! No spyholes, nor walls,
Nor cell-bars, nor the long endured pain –
Only a blue radiance on a tiny pane of glass –
A cast pattern – none more beautiful could be dreamt!
The more clearly you looked, the more powerfully
    blossomed
Those brigand forests, campfires and birds!
And how many times there was bitter cold weather
And how many windows sparkled after that one –
But never was it repeated
That upheaval of rainbow ice!
And anyway, what good would it be to me now,
And what would be the pretext for that festival?
Such a gift can only be received once
And perhaps is only needed once.[4]

What Irina and I have shared in common is the time to notice
these things in the context of suffering and pain, to appreciate
them and to let go of them. Enforced confinement was not our
choice but it was revealing. It highlighted the necessity of space.
Space makes sense of everything else. Without it, existence may
become meaningless or shallow.

(A year has elapsed since I first wrote this chapter. Returning to it again more recently I was overwhelmed with astonishment. I was struck by how the beauty of the light catching the ice on a tiny fragment of glass somehow outshone all the torture, deprivation and unbearable suffering of Irina's imprisonment. That's why the noticing of beauty and the delighting in its utter generosity, flamboyance and abundance must never be lost. These are the wonders that inspire us with the energy we need to respond as well as is possible to all the suffering that sometimes threatens to overwhelm.)

Working on this chapter I was conscious of the punctuation that creates pauses and sentence endings, enabling understanding of a text. I thought, too, of the rests and intervals in a musical score, and how these are essential to the way the music is played. In an exhibition at the Royal Academy the year before I became ill, I kept returning to a painting of a single silhouetted tree on a canvas most of which was space. I felt an expansiveness in its 'emptiness'. The Japanese talk about 'ma'. It is the space, for example, between the strings of a harp that enable them to vibrate and make music. The space is essential for the material substance to work. This idea permeates every aspect of Japanese culture and can be seen in such things as their minimalist interior design, and ikebana, the flower-arranging art where less is more. Space is not something one has to fill. It is what makes sense of things. Today many people feel they are on a treadmill of activity from which there is no respite. Others distract themselves from the uncertainty and uncomfortable complexities of life by endless noise of one kind or another.

St John of the Cross, a sixteenth-century friar and mystic, to whom my friend Rozzie redrew my attention, considered the first language of God to be silence. For me silence is the absence of words but not necessarily the absence of all sound: rather it is that experience in which the absence of distracting sound makes one conscious of the presence of all things, of being enveloped in, and part of the oneness of life. In a society where the tendency is to fill every available space – what is the fear that makes us do this? – we need to remember that space is what helps us to live fully, and we neglect it at our cost. No wonder many people feel stressed, confused, unsure how to go forward and, at worst, that life is a meaningless exercise to be endured, not enjoyed. We have been successful in 'normal' life at removing the one ingredient essential to our well-being.

At one level I think we are aware of this mistake. I notice how in more recent times mindfulness has become part of the lexicon and practice of people in the world of work as well as leisure. For centuries before mindfulness became fashionable, the major world faiths have held the value of quiet space or meditation, but they have also succumbed to the pressure to do and to speak far more than is good for them or anyone else. The Anglican tradition in which I was raised and became a priest has services so wordy that space rarely stands a chance, and how many times do people looking for a little quiet restoration enter churches only to be collared for yet more activity by welcoming but sometimes misguided members?

All this raises the question of what we fear might happen if we gave ourselves space simply to think and to be. It's often thought that those men and women who join contemplative monastic communities are running away from life. In reality most find the silence confronts them with all the awkward questions that life before becoming a monk or nun enabled them to ignore. We can run away from difficult situations and experiences but we always take ourselves with us. Unless we cut off emotionally from who we are, we cannot escape our complexities and confusions. If we cut off emotionally then we end up living a half-life, and never discover the wonderful gifts that come when we address the very contradictions and pains we want to avoid. So what might we encounter in times of space that makes us fearful of it? The first factor I want to consider is the realisation that we are not in control of life, and control is all-important to many of us.

3

Losing control

When I cleared my diary at the end of March 2017 and gave myself over to dealing with this lymphoma, the hardest thing to relinquish was control. I am generally very independent, and for a variety of reasons need to feel in control. I prefer giving to receiving, though inevitably I find I receive more from the wonderful people with whom my work brings me into contact than I think I ever really give. The situations that cause me greatest anxiety are those where I am dependent on others who leave me uncertain or keep me waiting for information that affects my well-being. Anyone who has experienced harm at the hands of others knows how hard it is to trust. The tendency is to maintain a sense of control, through healthy or unhealthy means and to seek belief systems – theistic or secular – which offer security and clear-cut propositions. It's a survival technique, often unconscious, suitable for emergencies perhaps, but not healthy in the long-term. Anyone or anything that raises questions about our position is cut out of our existence, or denigrated for being blind to the reality we have constructed. We end up restricting our lives instead of releasing them from the burden of past experience.

What was crucial for me as I went through abdominal surgery to confirm the lymphoma diagnosis, and then underwent intensive chemotherapy, was that I trusted the medical teams in whose care I found myself. This was because they were not only experts in their field but also treated me with the utmost respect and compassion. They kept me fully informed and explained every step of the journey. I would have struggled with anything less.

By 'trust' I do not mean I believe those I trust cannot fail me. Even the most trustworthy among us will at some point let someone else down. This may be because we are all human and fallible and we make mistakes, or it may simply be because our lives are committed to any number of people whose needs will take priority over the needs of others for whom we also bear some responsibility. My amazing specialist nurse, Mairéad, has been my strength and stay through this journey with cancer, but Mairéad's first priority is her family. She has consistently gone above and beyond the call of duty in supporting me through cancer treatment (and recovery), but she cannot always be there when I need her. Trust needs to be realistic. This is not only true in medical contexts.

I've noticed how unforgiving human beings can be when they feel let down by someone else. When trust is betrayed in any important relationship a common default position is to part company with, to split up from, or to divorce the offending party, as though we expect others to be perfect. Why do we expect perfection from others who, like us, are imperfect? Our imperfections may not be in the same areas, but they can be equally destructive, whether they cause an acute crisis or chronically eat away at a relationship little by little. There may be much that can be learnt from broken trust, not least a coming to terms with our own capacity not always to be what we aspire to be. I know of many long-term relationships that have grown and deepened, not because they were perfect but because the parties concerned have found ways to work with their flaws and failings, and the complexities of being human. They have chosen to be vulnerable and not to be in control as they move into the uncharted territory of another person's mind-set, their mindfulness and mindlessness.

As a teenager I saw human relationships in very black and white terms. I was judgemental in the extreme of anyone who fell short of what, as I believed back then, God demanded. I considered myself to be 'good'. I must have been insufferable! A lifetime of learning has taught me that, despite all the love in my life, and all the privileges and security, I am as capable of screwing up and hurting others as anyone else. It may rarely have been intentional, though I'm not immune from moments of wanting others to suffer for the hurt they've caused me, but I am always in the process of 'becoming', and failure and ignorance are inevitably part of that process. I have also had the privilege of working with and learning from men and women who have committed terrible acts of inhumanity in situations I can barely comprehend, and who have transformed their lives so extraordinarily that they are often at the forefront of teams working through the legacy of violence, despite still being regarded as 'the scum of the earth' by those who reject them. I trust, not because I believe my trust is invincible, but because I've learnt that even the most unexpected human beings may be transformed, and transform the toughest of situations, given the space and care to do so.

An image I found immensely helpful to the necessity of relinquishing control, or accepting I had little control when it came to this cancer, was brought to my attention by my friend Rowan. He told me that the Hebrew word often translated in the Bible as 'trust' is better translated as 'lie back on'. Although I am usually the one being lain back on, I could imagine myself giving in to the freedom of a deep sigh and falling back into the arms of people I trusted, who would hold me collectively through this debilitating experience. The image was more concrete than the difficult concept of 'trust' and enabled me to make the transition from needing to be in control to having very little control with much greater ease than might otherwise have been possible. I found a freedom in letting go, an experience only possible because of the teams looking after me, and the support of family and friends. This is why gratitude has been such a strong response in me since I've had cancer.

My gratitude also existed because I had access to such extraordinary treatments. I have sometimes worked in parts of the world where there isn't even basic medical care available, let alone the advanced technology, surgery and drugs required for the treatment of diseases such as cancer. So I found it hard to listen to people complaining in the UK about having had to sit and wait an hour beyond their appointment time to see the doctor ('and isn't the NHS awful'), when I thought how lucky we were to have doctors to see us, and care available that is beyond the wildest dreams of many people in our world. The privileges most of us enjoy in our society today seem to be so taken for granted that we are quicker to complain than to recognise just how lucky we are. Yet even as I noted this, I suspected the waiting time was not the core problem, only a symptom of the deeper issue, which was of not having control in the hospital situation.

I see also many men, women and children, here and abroad, struggling to get by without the help of family and friends, or anyone else for that matter, because in 'normal' society many of us have forgotten that the long-term well-being of any community depends upon it responding compassionately to the most vulnerable people in its midst. I suspect that the more reluctant we are to own our own vulnerability and lack of control in many aspects of life, the less open we are to the vulnerability of others. We do not want their woundedness to pierce the self-protective perceptions we have put in place to promote our belief that we are invincibly on top of things.

The desire to have a grip on existence, to feel we have a handle on the uncertainty and sheer riskiness of living, is utterly understandable. For the majority of the world's population the struggle for survival is a daily challenge. Trust is a risky strategy in a dog-eat-dog environment. It becomes important to know to which tribe I belong, where I can get any sense of security, who will enable me to get by for another day. For most people in the West, cushioned by material well-being, it is easier to park the fragility of life on the periphery of consciousness, and to trust the networks of family and friends we have built up. How differently might we live if we attended to the fact that life can and sometimes does go pear-shaped at any point, and all our security and certainty can fall away, exposing our vulnerability and helplessness?

The shock of this shift from going about our daily business with a sense of being in control to unexpectedly finding ourselves facing death is chillingly captured in Alden Nowlan's poem, 'The Execution':

On the night of the execution
a man at the door
mistook me for the coroner.
'Press,' I said.

But he didn't understand. He led me
into the wrong room
where the sheriff greeted me:
'You're late, Padre.'

'You're wrong,' I told him. 'I'm Press.'
'Yes, of course, Reverend Press.'
We went down a stairway.

'Ah, Mr Ellis,' said the Deputy.
'Press!' I shouted. But he shoved me
through a black curtain.
The lights were so bright
I couldn't see the faces
of the men sitting
opposite. But, thank God, I thought
they can see me!

'Look!' I cried. 'Look at my face!
Doesn't anyone know me?'

Then a hood covered my head.
'Don't make it harder for us,' the hangman whispered.[1]

The potential 'executioner' in my own case is this cancer. The year before I became ill, I loved my life. I was enjoying my work, and looking ahead to new possibilities. Now I not only have no idea what the future holds, I'm not even sure if I'll have a future. I, who have spent my adult life caring for others, am now dependent on others for care. I've asked myself, how could this be me? I've kept myself fit all these years, and valued being independent. I've been a 'giver' not a 'receiver', and preferred it that way. Now my life has been turned completely upside-down.

Few of us, I suspect, would willingly relinquish the feeling of being in control for exposure to this precariousness of life. Most of us, if given the choice, would prefer to be in the position of a certain rich young man who once approached Jesus asking what he needed to do to enter the Kingdom of Heaven:

Then someone came to him and said, 'Teacher, what good deed must I do to have eternal Life?' And he said to him,

'Why do you ask me about what is good? There is only one who is good. If you wish to enter into life, keep the commandments.' He said to him, 'Which ones?' And Jesus said, 'You shall not murder; You shall not commit adultery; You shall not steal; You shall not bear false witness; Honour your father and mother; also, You shall love your neighbour as yourself.' The young man said to him, 'I have kept all these; what do I still lack?' Jesus said to him, 'If you wish to be perfect, go, sell your possessions, and give the money to the poor, and you will have treasure in heaven; then come, follow me.' When the young man heard this word, he went away grieving, for he had many possessions.[2]

Here is a man, secure in material well-being and the accompanying power and freedom that often comes with wealth, who seeks Jesus out. Jesus speaks to him of the importance of keeping the commandments and the young man has them nailed. He may be a paragon of virtue or utterly deluded in his own sense of virtue, but the image portrayed is of one who has dotted all the 'i's and crossed all the 't's to living a successful life: a man in control of his existence. When Jesus says he must give up all his possessions to inherit the Kingdom, it is not the wealth in itself that is the issue, but the control, power and security these things give the young man, which he cannot relinquish. To enter a way of being that would put him in a position of not having control, of being confronted with the insecurities against which wealth protects him, to live with uncertainty, is a step too far for him, and, I suspect, a step too far for most of us to choose when we have other options. It requires a depth of humanity that we generally lack.

Who in their right mind would choose the way of helplessness and vulnerability? Yet these are conditions that can be experiences of sanctity and blessing. I mentioned earlier how, in his meditation

on the passion of Jesus, Vanstone shows that for the writers of the
Gospels of Mark and John the state of suffering, when Jesus moves
from doing to being done to, is the point when God's glory becomes
visible in him. In John's Gospel, when Jesus is arrested in the
Garden of Gethsemane, he asks the soldiers who they are looking
for and when they name him he replies with words that echo the
name of God revealed to Moses in the Hebrew scriptures, 'I AM'.
For a moment the soldiers draw back and fall to the ground. The
godliness of Jesus is not about power and might. He relinquishes
control for the greater purpose of inviting people into the Kingdom.
The Kingdom is a way of life lived in the here and now, where the
certainties and security we cling to are replaced by an expansive
and risky openness and responsiveness to existence and to those
with whom we share it. Kingdom values break down the barriers
that divide us, calling people into inclusive and costly community,
where the 'I' of the ego becomes the 'I AM', the mysterious 'us-ness
and other-ness' that is so much more than we can comprehend.

In his book *Goodbye to God*, Chris Scott recognises that the
words and images often used to give substance to our understanding of that which we call God inevitably fall short of what we're
trying to define. He suggests that traditional religious language
is no longer familiar to increasing numbers of people and, over
the centuries, it has accrued layers of interpretation that are life-
denying rather than liberating. He talks about 'living the dichotomy'
between subjective and objective experience. He describes this area
of experience as:

> . . . at one level unique to the individual, inasmuch as it has
> no empirically provable reference point (it is subjective);
> while at the same time this experience is held in common
> with others and appears to have an external source of being
> (it is objective).[3]

Because we cannot fully grasp this hard-to-articulate experience, we do not have control over it or what it may signify. Our ancestors understood this well. According to my friend Rabbi Professor Jonathan Magonet, when Moses asks to know the name of God at the beginning of the Exodus story, and God replies, 'I AM WHO I AM', God's essential message to Moses is to mind his own business because God cannot be pinned down and controlled any more than life can be.

What the story of the rich young man's encounter with Jesus makes clear is that when it comes to human beings recognising the limits of their control, and relinquishing it where appropriate, the renunciation must be voluntary. Jesus does not pressure the rich young man to give up the control he needs to live his life. He invites him simply to engage with this possibility.

Like the young man, I would never have willingly given up what I thought was my control of life. Of course, if I live to grow older, that discipline will be imposed upon me by the increasing frailness that comes inevitably with ageing. Yet we have imposed a certain expectation even on the elderly to be in control of their lives: value is attributed to those who 'remain active' in retirement and are not a 'burden on society'. After a lifetime of working there is still not quite the permission in our society to simply be, to be valued for who you are and not what you do. Loss of control of much of my existence had been imposed on me by illness sooner than I might otherwise have expected or desired. Yet I, who feared such a state and was not sure I had the courage required to be old, began to find a freedom and new sense of vision in it that was completely unexpected.

In Christian tradition perhaps the most well-known character to relinquish the control that came with privilege was St Francis of Assisi. For him, wealth did not provide the liberty he longed for. It bound him into ways of being that crushed his soul rather than setting him free. In his story we hear how he strips off in public the clothes that tie him symbolically to privileged family and duty, and mark his transition into a life of utter uncertainty, poverty, pain, joy and liberation. His journey is a 'Yes' to every aspect of living, not just the bits we'd like to experience, and it gives him a perspective on the suffering of others that, again, breaks down the barrier between 'Me' and 'Us'. St John of the Cross took the relinquishing of material and mental security even further. He wrote words I find hard, but also meaningful:

> To reach satisfaction in all, desire its possession in nothing.
> To come to possess all, desire the possession of nothing.
> To arrive at being all, desire to be nothing.
> To come to the knowledge of all, desire the knowledge of nothing.[4]

What I understand this to mean is that to have desire is to add 'I' to the equation – I want . . . – and therefore to impose one's own needs in a way that potentially becomes detrimental to the needs of others and prevents us becoming all we might be if we weren't dominated by personal desires for this, that and the other. Desire also brings dissatisfaction into the present, if the desire is not immediately met. I struggle with the words of St John of the Cross, but since I've been ill I've noticed how in being forced by this cancer to relinquish so many of the desires of my normal life, so much has come that is completely unexpected and not of my doing at all – the recognition of what really matters as opposed to what I thought mattered, connection with unexpected people, a sense of liberation despite the possibility that I might die sooner than I want to, the recognition of how much I have despite having lost a fair amount, the awareness of how much me trying to make things happen often gets in the way of them happening, and the astonishing realisation that when I step back from wanting to be anything in particular I seem to be someone others want to be with and opportunities emerge without feeling forced. Letting go of so much I thought important seems to have enabled a deeper sense of connectedness, which is less shaped by any desire for personal gain. All of which reminds me of Ann and Beth.

Ann and Beth both suffered from severe cerebral palsy. Neither was able to talk or control their body movements, nor convey that they were as mentally with-it as any young women their age, and probably more so. Both were wheelchair-dependent and needed full-time care. They were rangers, and we met at an annual camp where able-bodied and disabled guides and rangers came together for a week. Ann and Beth shared a room in the wooden hut on the campsite. One night between rounds, Ann was doubly incontinent. There was nothing either of them could do about it until the night staff came by but Beth managed deliberately to fall out of bed and judder across the floor between them so she could lie there and hold her distressed friend's hand while they waited for assistance. What immensely selfless and courageous empathy!

I experienced a similar compassion one early morning in hospital. I was in a bay of six women. Three of us would be dead before the year, or even the month was out; three of us hoped to be around a little longer. I woke on this particular day and found that every time I tried to sit up the world spun and I fell backwards into my pillows. I needed the loo but I couldn't even get out of bed. As I lay inert, wondering what was going on and how long I should wait to see if the problem lifted, I felt a gentle hand on my arm. Angela, for whom walking one step was a challenge at that point, had been aware of my struggling and struggled herself to get out of bed and bridge the gap between us to let me know I was not alone.

'If I can do anything to help, just tell me,' she said quietly, not realising that in that one effortful gesture she had already eased my sense of disturbance.

There's a troubling paradox in all this. I do not want suffering in the world. I do not want to suffer. I do not believe in a God who causes people to suffer. I see how suffering diminishes and destroys people, *but* I also see how suffering can build up and break open the human heart. I know from personal suffering and the suffering of others that without suffering in the world humankind would be less compassionate, less empathetic, less courageous, less aware of, and at ease with, its own neediness, less conscious of the joy as well as sorrow that exists in the valley of shadow. Men, women and children whose lives consist simply of being, of being 'done to', rather than doing, through no fault of their own, give as much to the world in that being, and perhaps do less harm, than those of us driven to egotistic action.

I became a nurse for selfish as well as altruistic reasons. I needed to be needed. My patients, quite unconsciously, met that need in me. One particular man, who wanted his next heroin fix more than my care for his deep vein thrombosis, in his rejection of my efforts to help him, confronted me with my previously unrecognised need. It was an important lesson because it enabled me to make sure I didn't allow that impulse in me to impact negatively on the care I gave to others in my work. I know from the nurses and health-care assistants on the ward today that many of their needs are met by the patients for whom they care. That's absolutely fine, so long as self-awareness prevents such needs sabotaging the potential for care.

I think too of baby Charlie Gard, whose story dominated the news as I was writing this chapter. He was born with mitochondrial DNA depletion syndrome, a terminal condition. His parents were fighting for the chance for him to have an experimental treatment in the States, while his medical team at Great Ormond Street had judged that he should be allowed to die and not be put through further suffering that had, in their understanding, no hope of success. Charlie was one of a number of babies in recent decades whose stories have reached a wider public because medical advances have created ethical dilemmas and heart-rending choices that we did not have to address in earlier times. These tiny souls will have no knowledge of the impact of their lives upon the thousands touched by their stories. Their existence causes us to reflect deeply on the value of a human life, the difficult questions that are part of the landscape which is the liminal space between life and death, what we can and should control and what we need to relinquish as we wrestle with the complexities of what it means to be human.

Beloved babies, like Charlie, highlight in a profound way what is true of all of us: namely, that in all the complexity of our ability and disability, whether that is physical or psychological, we affect the thoughts and feelings of others, the choices they make, the understanding, or lack of understanding, that develops between us. By our presence, those of us in more extreme circumstances confront others with realities they might otherwise be able to avoid, but from which they could learn a great deal.

Suffering is generally not a state to be chosen, but it is an essential part of life. Sometimes, for the higher cause of love, some will act in ways that they know put their lives and well-being at risk – the soldier saving a wounded colleague on the battlefield; the girl who speaks out for education and risks assassination in so doing; the woman who wills a world where compassion and community replace alienation and abuse of power and puts her life on the line to bring that about; the man who cares day in, day out for an incapacitated loved one, relinquishing his own aspirations because his love of that person makes any other option unacceptable.

I think what all this suggests is that we need to address the further fears that lie behind losing control of our lives and of recognising how in a moment we may move across the Styx from a life where everything was going as planned to a life where we have no idea what will happen from one moment to the next. Fear comes in many forms, so I want to consider some of its roots in the next chapter.

4

Facing our fears

Two days after I was discharged from hospital following my second chemotherapy, my temperature tipped over the 37.5 degrees mark. In normal circumstances this is a minimal rise, but for patients with cancer undergoing chemotherapy it is potentially significant. It required me to ring the oncology emergency helpline number. An hour later, following the advice of the nurses manning the hotline, I was in the Accident and Emergency department of my local hospital, in isolation and on intravenous antibiotics. Later in the day I was transferred to the hospital where my main treatment was taking place, having blood transfusions and being treated for neutropenic sepsis (a life-threatening complication of cancer treatment) and a *Clostridium difficile* gut infection, both of which had been triggered by the chemotherapy. Within the space of two hours I moved from feeling fine to being seriously unwell. When I first started writing this chapter I was having the same chemotherapy mix for my fourth treatment. It was likely the same complications would kick in and I'd feel rough and require hospitalisation. What was not part of this equation was fear.

Although I understood how serious the complications might be and how ill I would feel when they were at their worst, I was not afraid, precisely because I knew what to expect. Right from the time my diagnosis was clarified, my specialist nurse, Mairéad, was direct with me about the complications that were likely to come along the way. As a result, when they happened I saw them as part of the process of treatment, unwanted but not insurmountable, and I had the reassurance that others had experienced the same problems and come through them. So could I. Knowing what to expect was a key factor in enabling me not to fear what happened.

Fear of the unknown is, perhaps, the worst kind of fear. Those who torture others keep them in a state of not knowing what will happen and when. Those diagnosed with serious illness may live in a state of fear while they await news of treatment. Those caught up in the terror of violence or tragic accident may not always know what's going on, or what to do. Fear of the unknown, and our lack of awareness often of the exact nature of our fears, can be overwhelming.

In this chapter I want to touch on key fears that seem to dominate our lives, but before moving on to those, there are two aspects of fear that require mention. First of all, the fears that we have may have a basis in reality, or they may be figments of our imagination. In either case the fear can be debilitating. I venture to suggest that imagined fears which are never laid to rest can be far more damaging in the long-term of our lives than real fears we've had no choice but to face and address. In the case of real threat, fear is a key response. If we're able to channel it, it produces the energy required to physically fight or flee. Fear responses are part of our survival toolkit. Outside a survival situation, or where a threat demands a more considered response than fighting or fleeing, fear may be a less helpful reaction, and some fears can be destructive to us. They are the kind that wreak havoc in our psyches and find no resolution.

This brings me to my second observation about unaddressed fear. There's a story in three of the Gospels about a man who is racked by terror. In the understanding of his times his condition is described as demon-possession. Today I think of him as the archetypal embodiment of fear. I recognise 'him' as a voice within my own psyche from time to time:

> They came to the other side of the lake, to the country of the Gerasenes. And when he had stepped out of the boat, imme-diately a man out of the tombs with an unclean spirit met him. He lived among the tombs; and no one could restrain him any more, even with a chain; for he had often been restrained with shackles and chains, but the chains he wrenched apart, and the shackles he broke in pieces; and no one had the strength to subdue him. Night and day among the tombs and on the mountains he was always howling and bruising himself with stones. When he saw Jesus from a distance, he ran and bowed down before him; and he shouted at the top of his voice, 'What have you to do with me, Jesus, Son of the Most High God? I adjure you by God, do not torment me.' For he had said to him, 'Come out of the man, you unclean spirit!' Then Jesus asked him, 'What is your name?' He replied, 'My name is Legion; for we are many.' He begged him earnestly not to send them out of the country. Now there on the hillside a great herd of swine was feeding; and the unclean spirits begged him, 'Send us into the swine; let us enter them.' So he gave them permission. And the unclean spirits came out and entered the swine; and the herd, numbering about two thousand, rushed down the steep bank into the sea, and were drowned in the sea.[1]

The dynamics of fear embodied by the possessed man are all too recognisable. Fear can drive us into isolation, and into deathly places in our psyches. Unknown and unnamed, this fear cannot be fettered or silenced, nor is it open to the counsel of others. It makes normal life impossible. Sometimes we cling to our fear because, awful as it is, we are familiar with it. As Kafka observed, 'nobody ever shook a millstone from around his neck by complaining, especially when he was fond of it'.[2] That's why, in the story above, the fears of the man feel tormented by Jesus, aware he might reveal them for what they truly are, and thereby change the man's relationship with them. Like the man, we may recognise and value truth, but it torments rather than liberates us because what we need to do is to face our fears and bring the light of truth to them, and that may be more than we think we can manage.

Jesus asks the fear (unclean spirit) its name. In biblical tradition, to know someone's name is to know their identity. The name in this case is 'Legion' (meaning many). Unspecific fears have a wonderful way of multiplying to the point where living is a fear-filled endurance test. Once our fears are named, we have the possibility of taking control of them, of letting them go. Note, too, the amount of energy that such fears carry with them as this is expressed in the image of the broken shackles and chains and the 2,000 pigs surging into the sea. Think of how strong the possessed man must have been to contain these forces, and how much new energy will be available to him now he is freed from fear. In our own psyches the same is true. Fear faced can free up new energy for people to live more fully and not just survive.

This last observation is easily said and less easily lived, in my experience. Whenever I express any kind of fear my husband, Chris, has a habit of asking me to determine to what extent it is real or imagined. If it has some basis in reality the next question is whether or not anything can be done to address it effectively. If there is, then that must be done. If not then, along with any imagined anxieties, it needs to be kicked into touch. I understand the logic of this but many is the time I've wanted to poke Chris's eyes out as he says such things. It seems I am more prepared to sit with my fear than to release myself from it!

I want to turn now to the different fears that I have noticed play a part in the lives of many of the people I've encountered. As I have indicated, fear of the unknown becomes less fearful when the unknown is made known and understood, even if it involves pain and death. So what about the fear of death? It is a fear which took me to dark places in the past but over time has been laid to rest. This is not primarily a book about death, but any reflection on how we live our lives cannot help but address in some way our mortality. Our attitude to our own death and to the deaths of those closest to us will shape how we live. Those who fear dying often never live fully because they are haunted by the prospect of ceasing to exist, or of ending up in some kind of imagined hell. Others who do not value life play fast and loose with death, not caring if they should die sooner rather than later. How we accept our mortality determines whether we live fearfully, courageously, selfishly, blindly, openly, compassionately and so on.

One year, as a little girl on holiday in the stunning Highlands of Scotland, I remember being paralysed by the fear of dying. Why the fear suddenly arose in a place that I loved and where we were having fun, I have no idea. Perhaps being in a new and strange setting was sufficiently out of my comfort zone of home to provoke the questions that come to mind in childhood. I have it in mind that it was the thought of no longer existing that filled me with dread.

The thought of no longer being who I am distressed me sufficiently all those years ago that I retain the memory of it. One of my sisters, Pat, six years my senior, comforted me. I don't remember what she said but I know my fears were calmed, probably with assurances that I would live on after death: I grew up in a faith that assured me of life in heaven if I lived a good life before death. As a youngster I feared the threat of hell at times, but as an adult I have come to see images of life after death as the work of human imagination, attempts, perhaps, to find justice for suffering in the here and now – *you may not receive today the justice you deserve but it will come after death if not beforehand* – or a means of coping with the loss of loved ones – *one day we will be reunited.* These images have also been promoted as a means of exerting power over others – *do, or believe, things our way or else hell awaits you!* This threat of hell may be delivered in a threatening manner, or by people of a certain type of faith who express a genuine concern for your well-being as they tell you of the fate that awaits you if you don't follow the path they have taken!

When I was a student nurse, death was part of life. I nursed people in their dying days, watched them make the transition from life to death, and laid out their bodies reverently. Later, as a priest, I buried the dead and grieved with their loved ones. I know also what it is to face the fear of a partner or child dying from unexpected illness. Most recently, lymphoma has brought me into the shadow of death myself. I do not have the fear of the tortured or those for whom everyday survival with no hope of respite from poverty or disease is the norm. Their fear is not the fear of death but the fear of unremittingly grim life, and what others might cruelly do to them or how they may leave them to suffer. Should my present path lead to end-of-life care, rather than cure, I know the way will be eased by those who love me or look after me.

Today I do not feel the fear of death I once experienced. I may fear suffering in the lead-up to death, but not death itself. As I've grown older I've come to think death will be just the final letting-go in a lifetime of learning to let go – letting go of idealistic beliefs about the world and humankind as they proved unrealistic, letting go of dependence on parents as I moved into adulthood, letting go of perspectives and prejudices that proved wrong in the light of changing experience, letting go of attachment to things and expectations that I thought were important but learned were not necessary for a fulfilled life, letting go of loved ones who have died . . . and so on. In my time living with cancer, I've had to let go of many beliefs I had about my own identity and my worth as a human being, and though relinquishing attachment to beliefs or people can be hard, there is liberation in letting go. If I am lucky enough to have a good death I can imagine that my final breath might not be an 'Oh no!' moment but a peaceful 'Ah yes.'

Confronted by imminent and seemingly unavoidable death, terror may be the immediate and understandable response. Yet this is not the case for some with first-hand experience. Having faced what seems like certain death, perhaps on a battlefield or in a hospital bed, or in the face of an overwhelming and unexpected act of nature or terror, they speak of a sudden acceptance of the death they see as inevitable, a calmness that comes upon them unbidden after the initial terror. It is a *So this is it*, as their life flashes before them.

In our 'normal' society we are not healthy in our desire to hold death at arms' length. Though we often seek to pretend it is not, death is part of the warp and weft of life. It seems to me the border between the two is less clear-cut than we may imagine. Some people never really live, but stumble through existence, struggling to survive, or too shocked by experience to participate at anything more than a superficial level of engagement. In some communities the dead continue to live on through the lives of their descendants, or the rituals that bind the people to one another. Perhaps life itself is the minor reality. While I was thinking about death, my friend Melanie emailed an observation from Annie Dillard, 'Life is a faint tracing on the surface of mystery . . .'³ Maybe, at one level, we should sit more lightly to life, and to the mystery of death when it comes. I'm not sure this is something I would have suggested before having to face my own mortality with this cancer. Inevitably, until our own death draws close, our experience of it is second-hand, being alongside or watching from a distance the death of others. How we react to such deaths depends very much on the nature of the relationship we have with those dying. Where we are deeply connected it is hard, even impossible, to sit lightly to the death of a loved one. In his famous poem, 'Do not go gentle into that good night',⁴ Dylan Thomas rages against the dying of his father, but perhaps the latter wanted to go gently into oblivion, or whatever he imagined death to be. I remember my grandad being admitted to hospital in his nineties, not long after his wife had died, and him pulling out the drips the doctors kept putting in to keep him alive. He was ready to die. He wanted to be allowed to die peacefully and with dignity.

When I contemplate the death of those I love dearly, I am overwhelmed with grief at the thought of such loss, while the prospect of my own potentially earlier demise is one I accept now with little heartache, and even a sense of comfort. Because of the anguish that the death of others may trigger in us, it is hard to see death in anything other than negative terms, unless we have been faced with the reality and imminence of our own mortality. At that point it may take on a more comforting mantle.

I wonder to what extent our general fear about death, and our desire not to face it, lies behind the debate in our society at present about assisted dying? I hope medical advances will heal me of this cancer, but if they do not, I do not want to be kept alive for the sake of the beliefs of others, when my death is ultimately inevitable and my life has become a living death. I want a good death, pain-free, and surrounded by those I love, not long and drawn-out because society or medical practice dictates that such a death is a sign of failure, or cannot be allowed because assisted dying may be open to abuse even if carefully thought-through laws exist to prevent that, or is seen as making decisions only God should make (even though with the advent of medical science we have been determining whether people live or die for a long time).

One dominant thought that ran through my reflections about my own death was a sense of gratitude that I have lived a very full life. It made me wonder if part of the fear of death is really the fear of not having lived as we might have wished. What if each of us had to write our own epitaph or the eulogy spoken at our funeral service? What would we write? I wonder if the life I have lived so far is one that would be truly represented by the words I might want on my tombstone or spoken at my funeral. If not, what change is necessary now?

Regrets make death a harder road to travel. Being racked with guilt detracts from a peaceful death, unless you can see your past mistakes with the eye of understanding, not blame, and have done everything that can be done to put right the hurt you caused. This is not to let yourself off lightly, but to see the roots of harm inflicted on others in the context of your own woundedness, the life lived less than well in the light of the cards you were dealt in terms of genes, parentage, place of birth and privilege or poverty, and over which you had little or no control.

There are, thank God, only a handful of people I have met who have repulsed me. Yet when I listened to their story, while I could not accept their behaviours, or like the person they were, it helped me to understand why they had become that person. I was often left feeling, 'there but for the grace of God go I'. Kafka may have had the right sentiment when he wrote:

We are forlorn as children lost in the woods. When you stand in front of me and look at me, what do you know of the griefs that are in me and what do I know of yours? And if I were to cast myself down before you and weep and tell you, what more would you know about me than you know about hell when someone tells you it is hot and dreadful? For that reason alone we human beings ought to stand before one another reverently, as reflectively, as lovingly, as we would before the entrance to Hell.[5]

Compassionate understanding rather than condemning judgement seems to me to be far more the appropriate response at the end of life, our own or that of others. Who am I to judge harshly, knowing how, even with minor life challenges, I have failed perhaps to be all that I might be?

I know, also, that for me death will be harder if I come to it with relationships that mean much to me having unresolved loose ends. How many times have I heard grieving relatives express the wish they had told the deceased how much they loved them, or had sorted out a breakdown in that relationship before it was too late? Maybe in many, but not all situations, if we took the time and had the humility to address these broken relationships while those involved are still very much alive, painful regret would be one element we could remove either from our dying, or from our grief when a loved one dies. That we do not seek resolution before death may be due in part to another key human fear, the fear of rejection and alienation.

Most of us want to feel we belong, that there are people who love and accept us and will not desert us, but few of us experience truly unconditional love, and all of us to varying degrees will carry hurts that have determined the extent to which we are prepared to express who we truly are, and with whom. We may fall in with the expectations of family or friends or professional work patterns or social conventions, even if we'd like to live a different way, because the acceptance such acquiescence brings matters more to us, or is less demanding than discovering who we are beyond the expectations of others. Along the way we lose touch with the person we were or aspired to be – as Jackie Kay captures in her poem, 'Somebody Else':

> If I was not myself, I would be somebody else.
> But actually I am somebody else.
> I have been somebody else all my life.
>
> It's no laughing matter going about the place
> all the time being somebody else:
> people mistake you; you mistake yourself.[6]

It's also true that if we strike out for a different way of life from the one upheld by those whose acceptance matters to us, we may lose connection with some of them if their love for us is dependent upon us living 'their way', but we may gain new relationships with others who understand and affirm the life we are seeking to live. Part of the fear of rejection and alienation is of a lonely future. Why is it that in contemplating change it is sometimes easier to imagine the worst outcomes, than to picture positive possibilities? How many of us settle for unsatisfactory and unhappy present lives because we prefer to stick with what we know than to make changes which make the future less predictable and potentially more fearful?

Imagined futures can inspire or undermine present experience. Being visionary or having goals can influence positively the choices we make in the present, but an imagined painful future can impact negatively when played out in our minds in the present. For example, I was quietly writing this chapter when out of nowhere, or so it seemed, I was conscious of longing to live longer, and suddenly fearing I might not. The desire to live longer disturbed me. I thought I had come into a peaceful place by still waters that represented my acceptance of the possibility of dying sooner. The yearning to live longer added a grief to deal with, should it not be possible. This grief was of having to say goodbye and leave those I love dearly. I found myself imagining various scenarios and beginning to feel tearful. My active imagination was unhelpfully triggered by exhaustion, caused by the neutropenic sepsis, and by visits from both my children during that time. How much I loved them! How much I couldn't bear the thought of leaving them! How much I wanted to live!

In response to my expressed anguish my dear friend Richard sent the poem 'My own heart let me more have pity on', by Gerard Manley Hopkins. In its awkward and confusing structure as well as its words, it reflected back to me the disorientating impact of my tormented and distressed psyche:

My own heart let me more have pity on; let
Me live to my sad self hereafter kind,
Charitable; not live this tormented mind
With this tormented mind tormenting yet.
I cast for comfort I can no more get
By groping round my comfortless than blind
Eyes in their dark can day or thirst can find
Thirst's all-in-all in a world of wet.

Soul, self; come, poor Jackself, I do advise
You, jaded, let be; call off thoughts awhile
Elsewhere; leave comfort root-room; let joy size
At God knows when to God knows what; whose smile
's not wrung, see you; unforseentimes rather – as skies
Betweenpie mountains – lights a lovely mile.[7]

In sending me this poem I felt that Richard had heard my pain, taken it seriously and, in so doing, created a comforting space in which I could cry and calm down as pent up emotions found release and were laid to rest. This space enabled a lightness of being to break through into the darkness of my spirit, just as light breaks through between mountains.

From my own experience, and listening to many other people over the years, I know that many a moment of life is destroyed or overshadowed by the past living on painfully in the present – something I will return to in the next chapter – or a future that may never happen seizing our imaginations and running riot here and now. My imagination is a wonderful gift and sometimes a stumbling block. Caught by the past or possible futures, I have to work at noting the distraction and drawing myself gently back to the present, to the little picture of the north beach on Iona resting on my table, and to a ray of light that suddenly appears on the wall at the end of my hospital bed and gradually expands as the sun rises over the hospital, beyond my vision. Noticing and letting go, noticing and letting go. And if I do visit the future in my imagination, it doesn't have to be a negative or impossible one. I can shape positive outcomes. Steps into such futures might appear too large for me to take from my position in the midst of treatment, but every giant leap of imagination can be broken down into smaller actions that gradually effect change.

Research conducted by Macmillan and reported in the *i* newspaper on Monday 10 July 2017 showed that for one in ten people in the UK, fear of developing cancer is the biggest fear of all, ahead of losing a loved one, or dying or being a victim of terrorism. More and more people are being diagnosed with cancer, so fear is not unjustified, but survival rates are also increasing, with 50 per cent of those diagnosed between 2010 and 2011 surviving ten or more years. When you consider that 53 per cent of cancer deaths are in people aged seventy-five or over, fear of cancer may need to be tempered a little. Even as a cancer patient with an aggressive lymphoma at the age of fifty-seven, I do not think cancer is to be feared, but I recognise that for many of us it is only when we are given that diagnosis that we can begin to address our fear and perhaps find it is unfounded.

These fears, of the unknown, of death, of the life I'm leading, or rejection of past ghosts and future phantoms, are all linked by our sense of identity. It's to that subject I now turn.

5

Who am I?

'If I start to cry, don't stop: I want you to do this,' I said.

'I may cry too,' responded my husband, Chris.

He was standing beside me holding the hair clippers, about to give me a number one head shave. In a couple of days' time I was due to have my second chemotherapy, when all my hair would fall out. I had long, thick, blonde hair. I had decided to shave it all off before it came out in uneven clumps. I was not sure how this was going to affect me. In the past my hair has played a key role in my sense of who I am. I was conscious, too, that my ease or dis-ease with my body and how I looked had ramifications not only for me, but also for the people with whom my life connects and my attitude to the wider world of which I'm a part.

I was in my late twenties when, for the first time, I grew my hair long. To my surprise, as my hair began to inch down my back, I felt I came into myself as a passionate adult woman, as opposed to a little girl in a woman's body. It's not that the little girl disappeared. It's simply that I was able to own and express an adult dimension of my being that previously had not been given much air time.

Later, in my thirties, when my hair had grown to thigh length, I spent eight days in Auschwitz Concentration Camp with a group of Jews, Hindus, Buddhists and Christians. On the first day we were taken by a guide around Auschwitz 1. On the first floor of one of the barrack blocks, a third of the way across, a glass partition has been placed the length of the room. Behind it, piled up to above shoulder height, is human hair, the remains from the shaved heads and bodies of those transported to the camp, found when Auschwitz was liberated. More than anything else I saw, this memorial affected me profoundly.

In my forties I returned to the camp to record part of a programme I was making for BBC Radio 4 for Holocaust Memorial Day. I had interviewed a friend who had lost her hair as a result of chemotherapy for cancer, and she talked about the great impact this had on her sense of identity. I used the biblical myth of Samson and Delilah, in which Delilah cuts off Samson's hair, thus depriving him of his immense strength, to show how it illustrated the diminishing, strength-sapping impact of being dehumanised by others. Dehumanisation was one goal of the Nazis in shaving the men, women and children they sent to the camps.

While writing this chapter I was in a bay with four other women living with, or dying of cancer. One morning we had quite a discussion on the impact of losing our hair. Two of our group wore wigs, and one of the two spoke about how she would not let any of her family see her without her wig. She didn't know herself without hair.

'I cried when I first tried the wig,' she said, 'because I recognised myself again.'

The trauma of losing her hair echoes the experience of many friends who have spoken with me about this side effect of chemotherapy. As it turned out, much to my surprise, this was not my own experience.

Perhaps the impact was mitigated in part because rather than wait for my hair to fall out I chose to shave it off just before that happened. The daily sweats that are one of the symptoms of lymphoma always left my hair feeling claggy and damp. Once a permanent intravenous (PICC) line had been fitted into my upper arm at the beginning of my chemotherapy, washing my hair became a much more tiresome task because the PICC line (and, later, the Hickman line in my chest) needed to be kept dry. Washing my hair usually required me to kneel on all fours outside the shower, with my head inside so that Chris could shampoo and rinse my hair for me without the PICC line getting wet. It was undignified and uncomfortable. I reached a point where I wanted to be rid of my hair, no matter how I looked without it.

There were positives to having no hair: gone were the costs of hair products, visits to the hairdresser, waxing and plucking away unwanted growth. I could stand on a clifftop enjoying the wind blowing away the cobwebs without it also blowing hair into my face and turning me into a complete mess. For the first time in my life I found hats that fitted my head. The downside was that without eyelashes my eyes ran constantly when I was out in the fresh air, and my nose turned into a dripping tap. It was humiliating to stand at the checkout and find leakage running down and falling on my shopping before I could get a tissue out to stem the flow. At home I could wander around with rolled-up tissues stuffed into my nose, but it wasn't a look for public places!

Making the choice to shave off my hair before it fell out was crucial. I think a great deal of emotional pain is caused when we feel we have no choices, when circumstances beyond our control impose unpleasant experiences upon us. There was no question I was going to lose all my hair, but being able to choose how I lost it made a huge difference.

I notice that in everyday life all too frequently we disempower each other by removing the possibility of choice. Many of us are small cogs operating in big systems where decisions are imposed by those in power and we are required to implement them regardless of our own opinions about them. Think, too, of the survivors of the Grenfell Tower fire, who had the experience prior to the fire of their concerns about the fire hazards they saw in their block going unaddressed and then, in the aftermath of the fire, feeling, quite understandably, that they were not being listened to again, while others were making life-changing decisions about them and giving them little choice in what was being proposed. No wonder they were furious.

I'm conscious, too, of the pressure people feel to make choices so long as these don't put them at odds with those who hold greater power. In the Grenfell situation the survivors had nothing to lose in speaking out, but women and men working in big institutions can, and do, lose their livelihoods if they dare to expose unjust practices or unprofessional behaviours. We call them 'whistle-blowers'. We have some protections for them now, but not enough. Speaking truth to power is costly. It's another of those 'norms' in our society that some people in positions of power want to silence those who, in speaking out, highlight inadequacies in the system. Why do we accept this, or, if we don't accept it, do too few of us put our heads above the parapet to say that people who dare to challenge corrupt or inhumane systems should not be silenced or punished?

In shaving my hair off I discovered another reason why becoming bald was not the trauma I had expected: in doing so I did not feel any less me. Indeed, I felt confident enough to walk around without hats, turbans or wigs. Goldilocks became Baldilocks and, strangely, I was strengthened in that process. That may be because through the transition I realised I had become at ease with who I am, and my sense of identity and self-worth is not dependent upon how I look – although it's quite possible that if my teeth start falling out I might be less sanguine!

Along with the impact of cancer upon my body, and no longer being able to work or do many of the things upon which my sense of identity depended, losing my hair made me think about who I am, and *my relationship with my body*. Those final five words are instructive, as though I see my body as distinct from the 'me' I refer to as 'I'. Where did that distinction come from?

I grew up in a Christian family. My childhood was steeped in biblical stories and ideas that distinguished between body and spirit. I was taught that when my body died, my spirit, the essence of me, would live on. This caused an unconscious separation in my thinking between my body and me. What this understanding has meant is that I have seen my body as a tool, and one that I have pushed to the limits at times, in sport and work. True, I have enjoyed its speed and athletic looks, and I have delighted in its passions but I have not always taken care of it, or heeded its messages. For years, on the rare occasions I was unwell and my body wanted to stop, I simply carried on regardless, taking pride in my capacity to keep going, unlike weaker characters!

Yet the Ruth who ponders the relationship between herself and her body *is* this body. I am a creature with a brain that has the capacity to think and reflect. When I feel pain it is not my body that is in pain. 'I' am in pain. When 'I' make love I do not distinguish between mind/spirit and body. I am one with myself, even as I become one with another. When I experience psychological heartbreak I feel it physically in my guts. In other words, when I am living totally in the present moment, whether through pain or pleasure, I do not distinguish between my body and me. We are one – I.

As I sat in my hospital room contemplating who I was, it suddenly felt important to relinquish the dualistic understanding I had of my identity which distinguishes between my physical body and my spirit or the essential me, and to recognise myself as an extraordinary creature with physical and mental capacities, some of the latter of which I do not yet understand or use. Take my brain for example: given that our bodies are constantly replacing old cells with new, I wonder how those cells responsible for storing memories are able to 'pass them on' to new cells: How does that work? It is quite extraordinary. With Robert McCrum I find,

> . . . the idea that a brain surgeon must cut into thought itself, and through emotion and reason, is still mind-boggling. The idea that memories, dreams, and reflections should consist of jelly is beyond our ordinary comprehension.[1]

McCrum was brought to a profound awareness of his own physical being when, at the age of forty-two, he had a life-threatening stroke. The impact of the brain haemorrhage forced him not only to face his mortality but also to contemplate the nature of identity as physical disabilities impinged upon his self-understanding. Cancer prompted similar reflection for me. My need to resist a dualistic view of myself was because it created a hierarchy in my thinking which has been to the detriment of my body. I needed to redress that balance. If I understood 'I' to be my body in all its complexity and wondrous mystery, I decided I would treat it with better respect and care than I had perhaps done to date. I wanted to treat it as a subject, not an object. When I looked in the mirror and saw my wasted arms and legs, my bald head and my drug-induced pot belly bruised by the daily anticoagulant injections I had to give myself, I would, at last, see the beauty of a body that has been battered by disease and aggressive toxic treatment yet still walks tall, still laughs and loves.

In the past I've recognised this beauty in many people who don't conform to conventional images of beauty. Now I was learning to see it in me too. Our bodies are the storyboard of our lives. I don't want mine to be unmarked. As Almásy, the titular patient in Michale Ondaatje's, *The English Patient,* notes:

> We die containing a richness of lovers and tribes, tastes we have swallowed, bodies we have plunged into and swum up as if rivers of wisdom, characters we have climbed into as if trees, fears we have hidden in as if caves. I wish for all this to be marked on my body when I am dead. I believe in such cartography – to be marked by nature, not just to label ourselves on a map like the names of rich men and women on buildings. We are communal histories, communal books.[2]

All around us we see in the physical reality of those we encounter evidence of extraordinary stories, of pain and potential, lives lived to the full and lives lost along the way, myriad forms of being that in their imperfection still carry beauty, inspire transformation, speak of survival or trigger compassion. Posture, gait, mannerisms and physical presence reveal so much about who a person is, and how extraordinary they are sometimes, simply to have survived as they have. It's not that I don't appreciate classic images of beauty, but how lacking those are when the person who embodies them has little personality or depth. This perspective is counter-cultural in a society that, if television programming and general advertising are anything to go by, places so much emphasis on flawless superficial images.

At the time of writing, a series of *Love Island* on ITV2 had received a lot of attention in the media. This programme involved sending young men and women perceived as beautiful to a desert island with the purpose of them pairing off. It was superficial, mindless viewing from where I sat, and yet a significant number of people wanted to watch it. I wondered what it said about the lives of viewers watching, that this programme was the best they could do with the precious time they have. Perhaps it was pure escapism from difficult personal lives to watch supposedly beautiful people on a beautiful island, living the dream . . . or discovering that beautiful bodies are not enough and personalities may be much more complicated.

Another television arrival was *Naked Attraction* on Channel 4. The presenter invited participants to choose a date solely on seeing the naked bodies of other participants, which were revealed little by little. Both this programme and *Love Island* were on mainstream television channels. I have no issue with nudity in public. What I took issue with, apart from possible exploitation, were ideas of beauty that gave no sense of the stories that make us who we are, the personalities that create an inner beauty radiating outwards and that are not confined to conventional images of physical beauty.

Exploitation of our bodies comes in many forms. Sex-trafficking, pornography and modern slavery see human bodies as objects to be physically exploited regardless of the human subjects damaged or destroyed by such treatment. They are seen as bodies, not beings. These things are happening in our own supposedly civilised society, yet how many of us who do not want that to be the case take the necessary action to address this reality? It is not enough to say how awful sexual exploitation is, to be shocked when stories of organised sexual abuse of minors hit the headlines. If we know it happens but do nothing about it, we are complicit in it. As with so many abuses in our 'normal' society, it's the want of ordinary people speaking out and taking action to address them that enables them to persist to the extent they do. Ondaatje speaks truth when he describes our bodies as 'communal histories'. This is not just about genetic inheritance, but the relationships, both good and bad, which shape our experience in the here and now and leave their mark upon us. These may impose unacceptable pressure or prejudice upon who we understand ourselves to be. They may lack empathy. Empathy literally means, 'in-feeling'. It's about being able to enter into the being of another person, to understand their experience from the inside, in so far as that is possible. The separation I have described in myself, between mind and body, also exists between one person and another. We lose sight of the fact that we are interconnected, that who and how we are impacts on who and how others can be, and that the wounded or broken lives we encounter around us may be just as much a reflection on our own limitations of being as they are symptoms of some other person's or community's pain.

A simple example may be the extent to which in normal society we have created ideas of acceptable physical beauty that have contributed to teenage girls feeling ill at ease in their own skins because they don't conform to those images. Some develop eating disorders or other self-harming behaviours as a means of dealing with their sense of unease. Of course, there may be many factors which contribute to such disorders, but having worked with troubled teenagers in both comprehensive and public school education, I know how much the emphasis on physical beauty of a particular kind plays into troubled adolescent lives.

I wonder also how societal norms around beauty have led some older women and men to embark on plastic surgery that often leaves them looking artificial, rather than ageing gracefully, which has its own beauty. I note, too, those younger people who, dissatisfied with some part of their anatomy, have elective surgery to alter that aspect of their being. Do we want the kind of society that causes people to be ashamed of their physical being when it doesn't conform to the narrow definitions of beauty some have sought to impose? What messages do we convey about ageing and being old?

I know, too, that for some people who become significantly overweight, this development may be the means by which they've sought sanctuary from traumas such as sexual abuse, or is the result of dysfunctional body chemistry, or is a symptom of various other problems that have nothing to do with lack of willpower. Those who have felt they have the right to condemn obesity should perhaps reflect on the possibility that there may be more to a person's size than irresponsible eating, that the person they feel they have the right to criticise may be a survivor who doesn't need further abuse, verbal or otherwise.

How people feel about their physical being often affects their sense of identity and how the identity of others is perceived, the assumptions we make, the judgements we come to, the worth we ascribe or deny, and the relationships we are able to forge. The kind of insecurity that limits beauty to a certain flawless type of physicality may condemn those who understand who they are in very different ways from the alpha-male/girlie-girl stereotypes, particularly when those who do not conform to the stereotypes are in the minority.

I wrote much of this book in the year we marked the fiftieth anniversary of the decriminalisation of homosexuality in England. A great deal of positive change has happened, yet homophobic attacks continue to occur. Within my own faith tradition some people 'legitimise' their fear and prejudice concerning types of sexuality different from their own by attributing their views to God as they perceive God to speak through a particular interpretation of scripture. It's yet another symptom, I think, of our loss of connection with the fact that we are physical beings and that the human species is, quite naturally, full of variety. Science increasingly shows us evidence of our biological complexity and that gender and sexuality are a spectrum rather than binary in definition. My children take this spectrum as normal. They see the key factor determining the validity of a relationship being love, not heterosexuality, and whether people are healing rather than harmful in the way they relate to each other. They do not automatically think of difference as disordered or a disability. It seems arrogant for those who consider themselves normal to think they can determine what fulfilment and flourishing looks like for those who are different from themselves.

Illness, at last, has made me reflect differently about my physical being. Instead of working on my body, and making judgements about it as an 'outsider', I recognised I was an 'insider' working bodily with the insights, the insider awareness, this opens up. When we are at home in our own bodies, in all their miraculous complexity, we are much more at ease with the miraculous complexity of others who may be very different from ourselves. We are more likely to recognise each other as subjects to be respected, not objects to be criticised or abused. This does not mean we understand all things, or have no questions outstanding about what it is to be human creatures, but that we don't have to have everything sorted out. As Rainer Maria Rilke, poet and novelist, expressed it to his protégé, Franz Kappus,

> . . . be patient towards all that is unsolved in your heart and try to love *the questions themselves* like locked rooms and like books that are written in a very foreign tongue. Do not now seek the answers that cannot be given you because you would not be able to live them. And the point is, to live everything. *Live* the questions now. Perhaps you will then gradually, without noticing it, live along some distant day into the answer.[3]

Using Rilke's approach in relation to unanswered questions about what it means to be embodied human creatures brings me back to the art of living fully in the present moment, but with the added recognition of being in transition. I live here and now, knowing my understanding is partial, that life moves on, and that change is inevitable.

When we're living the present moment we are unselfconscious, totally absorbed in the present experience, not pondering it. Once we become self-conscious again, we are no longer in the present but reflecting on the moment that is past, or that is yet to be. Reflection, of course, is crucial. It's another reason why the mind/spirit and body split is so unhealthy for us. We are rational beings with the capacity to consider what we might do before we do it, and to reflect on what we have done with the potential of learning from it. We need to be mindful, not mindless. This mindfulness comes from a combination of thoughtful reasoning and emotional intelligence working in embodied balance.

As mindfulness has become fashionable in secular society – following in the footsteps of the major faiths that have been practising it for centuries – mindlessness seems to be increasingly apparent at all levels of society. While I was in hospital, undergoing my fifth chemotherapy, I was struck by an *Observer* magazine article about Al Gore. It prompted me to research Al Gore's perspective during my next admission for treatment. In his 2007 book, *The Assault on Reason,* Gore argues that the role of reason in American life and its politics in particular has diminished, with devastating consequences.[4] Much of his criticism relates to the administration of George W. Bush. He observes the manipulation of power by wealthy political funders, and the manipulation of truth by wealthy media moguls, in the context of the loss of the marketplace of ideas. In the latter space any person can test out the legitimacy of ideas, whatever sections of society they emerge from, through reasoned argument, and not forgetting emotional intelligence. He writes about the need to find new ways to have a meaningful non-manipulative conversation about how life should unfold. In such a conversation the rejection and distortion of substantiated scientific facts is no longer tolerated. There is an end to false information being created and utilised by big businesses or politicians to cloud the issues and make it difficult for the general public to discern what is true and what is fake. He cites many examples of American life at the time to show how

> Greed and wealth now allocate power in our society, and that power is used in turn to further increase and concentrate wealth and power in the hands of the few.[5]

He writes about how politicians have fuelled fear rather than generated understanding in order to manipulate public opinion, and he speaks of fear as 'the most powerful enemy of reason'.[6] When it comes to leadership, Gore writes:

> Leadership means inspiring us to manage through our fears. Demagoguery means exploiting our fears for political gain.[7]

If what Gore says about American life and politics back in 2007 contains truth, and I found his arguments compelling, it could be argued that his words are even more pertinent today when people struggle to distinguish between fake news and facts, and reasoned dialogue involving all people regardless of wealth or status is too frequently replaced by diatribe and appeals to fear and prejudice. The UK parliamentary system doesn't set a good example, with MPs facing each other across the divide seeking to demolish each other's positions, not with informed and reasoned reflections but with insults and exchanges of statistics, the truth of which is hard for the average person to verify. Some users of social media feel they have licence to verbally abuse and threaten others whose views are very different. They seem unable to argue their own case with intelligence, drawing instead on insults and threats. On TV debate programmes, the belief that pitting people against others with deeply opposing views makes for good viewing, and the limitation of time given to serious issues, means that there is rarely worthwhile debate or the seeking of constructive ways forward given the differences that exist. These are 'norms' I don't accept. It's not the kind of society in which I want to live, because it reflects how fragmented we have become.

Ian Hamilton Finlay, the creator of one of my favourite gardens in Scotland, Little Sparta, wrote that, 'FREEDOM OF SPEECH IS NOT FREEDOM TO SPEAK IT IS THE FREEDOM TO DISCUSS'.[8] His distinction is critical in my understanding. There appears to be an assumption that freedom of speech means being free to say whatever you like regardless of the destructive consequences for other people. The desire to speak freely must be rooted in a commitment to coming to the table with sometimes widely diverse and conflicting views with the purpose of trying to find a creative way forward. It means being able publicly to stand by what you say, not to hide behind anonymity or to say things across cyberspace that you would not dare to say to someone's face. Freedom of speech is not about dumping your views on others without taking responsibility for them and for finding a better future.

Just before I had to give up work due to this illness I was running a training workshop for a group of Iraqi leaders. They spent a morning working with international journalist Jack Merlin Watling. Alongside his significant journalistic achievements, Jack has worked in many communities teaching public-speaking and debating skills to enable people to learn how to articulate their concerns and grievances effectively. It is one way to help those who often feel they have no voice to speak out. Part of the process invites those participating to give arguments supporting the view with which they disagree. The purpose of the process is not only to enable a person to articulate clearly their own viewpoint but also to see why another person might understand a situation very differently. It is one way to help people rehumanise those they have dehumanised through conflict, and to begin to address the alienation arising from the psychological distance between individuals and communities.

I know from my own work mediating conflicts and facilitating difficult conversations that each of us only has one or two pieces of the jigsaw of human experience. We need to hear and understand why others hold their particular position, and the experiences, fears and hopes that lie behind it. Understanding doesn't mean we agree with what we've heard, but it does help to build the bigger picture and to enable more informed decisions. Much was made during the 2017 UK election campaign of the fact that Jeremy Corbyn, the leader of the Labour Party, had talked with the terrorist IRA in the past. This was an action those raising the matter thought wholly unacceptable. While questions of the timing of such conversations are important, those of us who work in the field of conflict transformation know that in most violent conflicts, at some point or other, the people in conflict need to sit down and talk to each other, including the men of violence. That's why the seemingly gentle beatitude – Blessed are the Peacemakers – is such a challenge. We may be asked to bless the very people we consider to be our enemy once they come to the table to talk peace. It's so much more comfortable to see these situations in terms of goodies and baddies, but such a worldview belongs to the realm of child's play, not adult engagement in a complex context. The Good Friday Agreement in Northern Ireland would not have come into being if such conversations had not happened, often in secret, often in monasteries or church centres where there was wisdom enough to recognise that if you are called to bless the peacemakers, that will require dialogue with the warmongers without whose involvement there can be no prospect of peace, unless a stronger armed force defeats them in conflict.

Non-communication through diatribe, rather than dialogue, or converting you to my opinion rather than conversing with you to seek mutual understanding, are norms in our society which need to change. How can we be mindful if our minds are full of assumptions about the 'other' that we've never tested out, and we never find the right time and space to properly listen to the experience of others whose worldview is very different from our own?

In the light of my reflections about my body, Al Gore's writing not only made me think about the balance of heart and mind in our engagement with others, but also how the unease people feel about their body and their body's passions may affect how we treat planet Earth. I think a valid comparison can be made between the mind/body split I've written about in this chapter, and the humanity/environment split with which we are increasingly wrestling today. We are the dominant cause of climate change and, as Al Gore writes:

> The edifice of civilization has become astonishingly complex, but as it grows ever more elaborate, we feel increasingly distant from our roots in the earth . . . We now dare to wonder: Are we so unique and powerful as to be essentially separate from the earth?[9]

For many years I have been able to think of climate change as something that affects other people far from my own home environment. It disturbs me but doesn't directly affect me. More recently a community I work with regularly in Egypt helped me to see how the Mediterranean is encroaching on the fertile plains of the Nile Delta and the sea water is slowly taking land that is the bread basket of Egypt. Already this is adding to instability in the country. They made me realise how complacent I have been, and how my sense of disconnection with my body, with wider humanity and with the environment has blinded me to the interconnectedness of all these things.

The impact of climate change is well documented. It is not new science. During my gap year, as hurricanes Harvey, Irma and Maria laid waste to the islands and cities they passed through and I tried to take on board the statistics and evidence indicating the damage we are doing to the Earth, it struck me forcibly that as a species we are sleepwalking our way to devastation and disaster. Lying awake on the ward one night I found myself thinking that if I died sooner rather than later I would not be around to witness more wars resulting from communities fighting for increasingly scarce resources like water, and mass migrations triggered by the spread of the desert or the loss of land to the sea. These things will surely come if we continue mindlessly down the road we presently travel with regard to climate change.

It is not simply that people are ignorant of, or indifferent to, the damage for which we as a species are responsible. There are news items about how businesses whose profits result from highly polluting practices have sought to put out misleading information designed to undermine what the majority of environmental scientists say is true. Sometimes uninformed voices are given airtime they do not have the expertise to deserve. As I was writing this, a controversy broke out about a debate on BBC Radio 4's *Today* programme in which Al Gore was questioned alongside climate-change denier, Lord Lawson. The BBC initially defended their decision to include Lord Lawson as part of their duty to inform listeners of all sides of an argument. This is about balance, but is it balanced to give equal attention to a view that by the majority of scientific evidence is discredited? (The BBC have since acknowledged that accuracy and impartiality were not well served in the interview.)

Donald Trump's withdrawal from the Paris Climate Change Agreement in 2017 flew in the face of all the scientific evidence that had made the Agreement a necessity. The Agreement, signed by 159 nations in December 2015, and which came into force in November 2016, lays out commitments for signing nations to limit their greenhouse gas emissions with a view to lessening and containing the impact of global warming. It is a measure of the mindfulness of other leaders that they did not follow Trump's example, and that many cities in the United States are choosing to ignore their President's decision and will continue to work to fulfil the commitments of the Agreement which relate particularly to cities.

In the same way as I saw myself as somehow separate from my body, which was relegated to being a tool or resource I didn't always use well, humankind seems to have lost sight of the fact that we are not separate from the Earth. As Gore goes on to write, 'The problem is not our effect *on* the environment so much as our relationship *with* the environment.'[10] We are one species among many upon it. We are interdependent. We are part of it.

At one level we live in a society where we are seemingly more relaxed about bodies and bodily functions and, one way or another, display them more than has been the case in previous generations, yet we continue to relate to them in a disembodied way. Rejecting the dualism of body and spirit has been an important step for me to take, but it leaves at least one loose end: what about those experiences which seem to be about more than my physical reality? Jung talks about the collective unconscious, which is so much more than an individual's consciousness. There are times when I feel connected to an active energy affecting my life that is more than a human creation. I'm struggling here to articulate it, and yet it is part of my experience. As I worked my way through cancer treatment, reading what came my way as I went along, my thoughts around this subject developed further and found expression in Chapter 7 ('To be or not to be . . .'). As I head in that direction I want to explore the storylines that shape our identity and the extent to which we can change them and reshape who we are.

6

Separate and shared storylines

So far I have expressed the understanding that separation is a negative aspect of human experience. Early on in my gap year Paul Tillich's reflections on separation made sense to me.[1] He notes how, over the centuries, the word 'sin' has been subject to distorting interpretations that have undermined its power. The word that he suggests might reconnect us with the nature of sin is 'separation', that destructive state of being in need of the redemptive power of grace to restore oneness and wholeness. It will be clear from my last chapter that I felt very much in tune with the understanding of separation as profoundly destructive to human well-being, but this is only one strand of the storyline thread of separation that has run through my experience of cancer.

Between my fifth and sixth chemotherapy sessions I had a weekend out of hospital that enabled me to spend a day with my daughter, Freya, my son, Tian, and Freya's partner, Aled. It was our first visit to see Freya and Aled since they'd moved into their new home right by the River Thames. We sat on their lovely balcony and watched the people enjoying that particular Sunday messing about on the river in all kinds of boats. Tian had not long celebrated his twenty-first birthday. The previous evening Freya had given him a book she'd compiled for this special occasion with photos and messages from all the family and friends who have been important to him in his life so far. There were lots of photos from when he was a baby and little boy. I'd taken several of them, but had quite forgotten about them. Freya had deliberately put in lots of positive images. Tian was both hard work *and* a joy to raise, but sometimes the prevailing message he picked up was 'hard work' not 'joy'. 'Hard work' is not the predominant storyline we want him to take into adult life. He is a joy to us.

All of us inherit storylines from our key carers and past experiences. Communities as well as individuals inhabit storylines passed on from one generation to the next. For good or ill these stories shape our sense of identity. It feels very emotional looking back to times which were clearly a lot of fun, and to remember the joy the children brought us as they grew up, but being with Freya and Tian has made me more emotional than any other aspect of living with cancer. I know this is because it's at such moments that my 'normal life storyline' connects with, and gets tangled up in, my 'walking through the shadow of death storyline'. I can inhabit each story on its own but I feel at my most vulnerable trying to hold the transition and tensions between the two. When I am with my children I am most acutely conscious that I may not be around to witness the futures they are unfolding for themselves, and the thought has grieved me deeply.

When Chris and I arrived home after our day with Freya, Tian and Aled, I couldn't settle to anything. I felt tearful. I snapped at Chris and in the end I took myself off to bed early because I knew my mood was not to do with him at all but expressed my struggle to weave together 'normal' life and being treated for a life-threatening illness. I've learnt that in order to navigate this difficulty, there are times when I need to separate myself from those closest to me.

In some ways, this is a continuation of how I have dealt generally with personal problems in my life thus far. I tend to 'batten down the hatches' and go into solitary mode. I want to focus without distractions. I love my husband and children dearly, but as I have worked my way through cancer treatment, there have been times when I've needed to be on my own physically, separate from them, and separate from all the friends I have. It is lovely having people who care about me, but at times it could be overwhelming receiving so many messages asking me how I am, at moments when I felt least able to respond. Apart from questions from those most close to me, the loveliest messages were those which didn't ask questions, but included photos of beautiful scenes or flowers, or sent love without requiring a reply; not that I always read them the moment they pinged into my inbox. Sometimes I've simply needed to be alone.

There are some experiences in life that we can only address on our own, although we may wish others had the answers for us. Having solitary space to reflect on what's happening, or just to 'be', without distraction, is as important for me in this journey as all the medical intervention and the support of family and close friends. Getting the balance right between separation and relationship isn't always easy. I wonder if it's harder for my children's generation and those born after them, growing up with information technology that enables them to be constantly in touch with others. My observation is that those whose need is to be continually online are often disconnected from any meaningful sense of self, and superficial in their social media contributions. As Jean Vanier, the inspiration behind the L'Arche communities, says, 'We've become experts in communication, but we're not so good at presence.'[2] Paradoxically, I think our difficulty in being present to others is rooted in our unease with being alone with ourselves. There is a state of separation that is crucial for growth and development. To know myself separate from others is just as important as understanding my oneness with them.

We come into being through the union of one person with another, but immediately a sperm and egg come together one cell becomes two, two become four, four become eight and the division continues into a multiplicity of cells that differentiate and take on their own particular identity, separating off from other distinctive cells and yet united in the whole, each dependent on the actions of the others. Through birth a baby becomes a distinct being, dependent initially on their parents or key carers but also separate from them. Every stage of development is geared towards children learning to stand on their own two feet and to live life as fully as possible. They may be supported by those who raised and love them, but they do not live in their shadow.

When I left home, aged nineteen, to train as a nurse, I moved from a small market town into central London. My whole world opened up. People about whom I'd held black and white views, but never knowingly met, became fleshed out human beings, people I cared for, or worked with on the wards, or met as I explored the city and became part of a community in Elephant and Castle. I arrived in London with a whole range of storylines about myself and others, essentially inherited from my parents, or formed within a very limited sphere of personal experience. Leaving home gave me the opportunity to begin to work out who I was, how far, if at all, I shared my parents' understanding of me and the world, and the storylines I wanted to continue to weave through my unfolding experience.

As I was working on this chapter my dear friend Alison dropped the word 'haecceity' into my consciousness. Apart from struggling to know how to say it (I think 'heck-SEE-ity' is the way) I also had no idea what it meant, but she thought it relevant, so I set about doing some research on it. It arises out of the thinking of Duns Scotus, an important thirteenth-century philosopher/theologian. Haecceity is that which makes a thing essentially itself, distinct from every other thing. It is its 'this-ness'. 'Haec' means 'this' in Latin. It's what makes me uniquely Ruth, as distinct from one woman among many women, for example. Understanding my 'this-ness' comes about as I understand my inherited storylines, reject those which no longer make sense of my experience and create new ones, integrating the old and new narratives that make me 'me'. The more I draw into consciousness, the more I can understand what my story has been, and choose what I want it to be now. Jung talked about this integration as individuation. In the process we learn who we are, not only as distinct from others, but also in relation to others, because the conversations of individuation or understanding our this-ness, arise out of or within relationships, and are often a dialogue (internal or external) between the storylines we have inherited, the stories of our present experience, the stories we want to be our present, or assume will be our future, the storylines we remember, reject, rework, and invent or reinvent. When the writer Irvine Welsh was about eight or nine, his father went into a coma. Reflecting on that experience he says, 'I think it encouraged me to go into my own imaginative space. When the narrative of your own life is uncertain you build alternative narratives.'[3]

A number of times during my treatment I have needed blood transfusions. As I watched the blood dripping in the intravenous line I thought of the people who'd given their blood which was now becoming part of me. In my imagination I thought of how, like these transfusions, we take into ourselves all kinds of storylines that key people in our lives give us, intentionally or unintentionally. I mentioned at the beginning of this chapter how one storyline my son may have of himself is of being 'hard work'. Hopefully, he has many other storylines in his conscious memory, like being a joy to us, that are infinitely more positive and which enable him to understand the 'hard work' storyline in context and not give it more prominence than it deserves, thus preventing it sabotaging the storylines he creates in the present and future.

It's important to understand at this point that memory is not a replaying of past history. Memory is an interpretation of the past filtered through our dominant storylines, conscious or unconscious. As I was writing this chapter during my sixth four-day chemotherapy in hospital, my friend Rosie sent me a book, *Burn After Writing*, a frivolous or thought-provoking book depending on how seriously you take its invitation to answer in writing as honestly as possible all kinds of personal questions which determine our identity. Near the beginning, with reference to the past, it reads:

> Maybe you can't change what actually happened, but the way you remember it is never the same twice. Every time we remember something, we relive it from a different camera angle. We always reinvent our history to suit our present need.[4]

There is much truth in this. Whenever my family is reminiscing over past times it always astonishes me the different things we remember about the same experiences, sometimes to the extent that I wonder if we were at the same event! This is not to say there are no facts in what we remember, but my interpretation of my past and my relationship with others is always *my* interpretation. I think it's accurate to what actually happened, but the interpretation of others who were there may throw that belief into doubt, or at least indicate that memory is more complicated than we generally recognise.

Memory, of course, is all we now have of the past, unless we have it captured on camera, and even that will only be from certain viewpoints. How we understand what's gone before may change as our present experience evolves. We re-member, put back together, the facts of what happened according to the storylines we're running. If, for whatever reason, we have negative dominant storylines, such as, *I am useless, worth nothing and will amount to nothing*, we tend to remember those experiences in our lives which prove these storylines, and we reinterpret positive experiences in the present through a negative filter: *It was a fluke; anyone could do that; other people made it possible; I couldn't have done it on my own.* The stories we inherit and the expectations we have as a result of the storylines we play out in our lives may blind us to new possibilities and keep us stuck in old patterns that may or may not feel safe, but are certainly stifling.

One more point about memory: Sometimes our memories are not even *our* memories. As Hilary Mantel writes of one of her characters:

> In later life, the child Georges-Jacques thought he remembered his father. In his family the dead were much discussed. He absorbed the content of these conversations and transmuted them into what passed for memory. This serves the purpose. The dead don't come back, to quibble or correct.[5]

Sometimes it's impossible to distinguish whether my memory of a past experience is my own memory or the memories of others that I unconsciously absorbed as a child, hearing the stories those close to me told about my exploits or the actions of other family members. Just a few days ago, Chris and I had a short break in Dorset in preparation for my month in the Isolation Unit. We visited Lulworth Cove, a place my own family came to when I was a toddler. It had a warm, familiar feel, but that may simply be because I've seen photos of it in the family albums and heard my parents talking about it.

Whatever our memories suggest, the storylines of our identity are not set in stone. Sometimes we can see their evolution in the names we have been called over time. It's worth pausing for a moment to think of all the forenames, surnames, nicknames, professional titles, misnomers, even fleeting indicators (for example, for the nurses on the ward where I've spent a lot of time, alongside being Ruth, I am 2.2, the reference to the bay and bed I occupy) we have collected since birth, what they say about our identity, whether they have positive or negative connotations and what we feel about them.

It's interesting to note what names we think reflect who we are, and what names we want to abandon. I was christened Hilda Ruth, but was always called Ruth and never felt Hilda was me. In my twenties I changed my first name by deed poll to what my mother had wanted it to be – Helen Ruth. It felt more me. In biblical tradition key figures receive new names to mark their change of identity, or the recognition of some aspect of being that needs breathing space. Simon Peter, one of the disciples of Jesus, became Peter the Rock after a flash of inspiration broke through his general clumsiness and lack of clarity. As he tried to follow Jesus, this fisherman was all at sea with the changes in his life, but there were moments when he stood on surer ground and saw the possibilities that his new life opened up for him. It's not that he was suddenly a sterling character, but the name Jesus gave him recognised an aspect of his being into which, once recognised, he could grow more fully.

When Mary Magdalene encounters a gardener after the resurrection, she recognises the presence of Christ only when the gardener says her name, recognising her personhood and treating her with compassion. Working with gang members in Los Angeles in the present day, Gregory Boyle, a Jesuit priest, expresses how crucial it is to learn quickly and remember the names of the gang members with whom he shares his life and work, and how finding the right name can recall these people back to the selves they had lost through violence, shame and despair. He speaks of pressing one young man for his most meaningful name, not the name that invokes his violent reputation, or his surname, or his formal first names. Eventually there is a transformation in the youth's defensive swagger and sneering attitude.

> 'Sometimes,' – his voice so quiet, I lean in – 'sometimes . . . when my mom's not mad at me . . . she calls me . . . Napito.' I watch this kid move, transformed from Sniper to Gonzalez to Cabrón to Napoleón to Napito. We all just want to be called by the name our mom uses when she's not pissed off at us.[6]

In these examples, names are crucial to a person's sense of individual identity, but they arise from our relationships with others, and say much about the storylines we inhabit and how these interweave with those who have the greatest impact on our lives, for good or ill.

When I used to conduct weddings I always asked the couples coming to me to think of a book, TV programme or film that best gave a flavour of their life before they met each other. When Chris and I did the same thing years ago, he came up with Charles Dickens' *Bleak House* and my choice was Enid Blyton's *Famous Five*. The very different choices illustrate well the different storylines brought into a relationship, and the challenge of creating the storyline of the unfolding marriage relationship, developing new aspects of identity from distinct stories in such a way that individuality is not suffocated but able to flourish in the shared life.

The wisdom is that 'I am' because 'we are'. Healthy separateness depends upon healthy relationships, and vice versa. The African concept of 'Ubuntu' describes how 'a person is a person through other persons'. Just as the blood I've received from others over recent months becomes indistinguishable from my own blood so, too, the uplifting stories of others may become integral parts of my own narrative, and others may take into themselves aspects of my story they find restorative.

When I felt a bit feeble in relation to this cancer, my mum's example of courage in the face of debilitating symptoms strengthened me: *This is how I want to be strong*. When the daily injections I needed to put into my abdomen increased at one point from one to three every day, I thought of my son Tian who, as a Type 1 diabetic, has been injecting himself with little complaint several times a day since he was eight years old. These are simple examples of how the threads of other people's stories become embedded in the fabric of my being, the warp and weft of my own responses.

At other times, as I become aware of them, I can tie off a storyline I think is unhelpful, and introduce a new thread. I think change, individually and communally, is essential when it comes to some of the stories we're living. From the societal perspective I wonder, for example, if we have lost some sense of the connection between being individuals and being in relationship, of being separate and of being part of one another. Looking at normal society from the shadow of death it is hard to avoid a sense that many of our dominant storylines are selfish rather than self-giving:

- Financial and material security is only for the few at the expense of the many.
- Every person or tribe for him/her/itself.

- What you do rather than who you are is the measure of your worth.
- We don't want you around because you're too different from us.
- Short-term greed over long-term generosity.
- We are destroying the Earth but we're too selfish or blind to change direction away from the disaster we're creating. This is how it is; change is not possible.

I've picked some negative messages because these are the ones that leap out at me, and because these are the ones that dominate our twenty-four-hour news channels and newspapers. I question the need for round-the-clock news, and what it does to us constantly to hear terrible stories, most of which we can do nothing about. The pressure on those who bring us the news to fill the space leads to ridiculous situations. One morning in hospital I listened to a well-known radio presenter reporting the bombing of the tube train at Parson's Green station in London, just after it had happened. For the rest of the programme he was talking to people at the scene, or who were experts on such incidents, speculating about what had happened, how many might have been killed or injured, and who was responsible. His listeners rang in with comments, and all this happened before all the facts were known. It seemed like madness, with everyone getting fired up before they knew for sure what there was to get fired up about. The speed at which we live today may fuel problems rather than take out the heat from them.

There are two relevant stories in gospel tradition where people are racing along on high emotion, and Jesus pushes the pause button. In the first story one of his close friends, Lazarus, has died. The sisters of Lazarus send messages to Jesus begging him to come immediately, but he delays going to the family. It seems heartless, but the effect is to inject a breathing space into the grief. He makes room for his own grief so that when he eventually comes to them, he is able to bring a different dimension to their experience – to bring life out of a death-dealing situation. In the second story a group of outraged men bring to Jesus a woman caught in the act of adultery. The punishment is stoning, but they want to know what Jesus thinks, perhaps to trap him. Putting aside the injustice of the adulterous man apparently not receiving the humiliating treatment meted out to the woman, Jesus' reaction to the emotionally aroused men clamouring for action is poignant and powerful. He doesn't leap in with a response. He doesn't allow himself to get caught up in the emotion swirling around him. He doesn't stand eyeball to eyeball with the men. He bends down, seemingly taking a non-threatening, even submissive, position, and writes in the sand. He says nothing. His action and silence still the men down. The group dynamic of aggression and self-righteousness is drained away as they strain to see what he's doing, and to hear anything he might say. When he does speak, they are able to respond thoughtfully to his comment, 'Let him who is without sin, cast the first stone.' Instead of judging the woman, they are asked to look to their own behaviour. Without the 'pause' I doubt they would have been able to do that, and the story would have had a very different ending.

In my work as a mediator and facilitator, being able to hold quiet space is as essential as being able to ask the right questions. I need to avoid getting caught up in the heightened emotion that people often feel when they come into a mediated but difficult conversation. I feel the same need to hold some kind of emotional distance from the barrage of bad news that assails us today. For that reason I limit the amount of news I listen to, watch or read. I need to be informed in order to take the action I need to take, but I also recognise there are some things I cannot address. It's a challenge to get the balance right between fulfilling my responsibility to build up our common life, and not feeling paralysed by the enormity of the task. I wonder whether, if each of us tried simply to change positively our own storylines, life more widely would gradually get better. We don't have to wait for others to make changes.

The extent to which change is possible depends upon the stories we choose to tell about who we are, the stories we buy into, the stories we want to hear regardless of whether they reflect reality, whatever that is, and the way we work with the stories we inherit or which are part of wider society. I am conscious as I write this book that I have dwelt on the bad news of human life more than I've focused on the good. The purpose of my writing has been to highlight the dysfunction I perceive in normal life as I walk in the shadow of death, but in so doing I have edited out the many stories I could tell of amazing individuals and communities whose examples of courage, compassion, generosity, perseverance and sheer good-heartedness make the world a better place than the media would generally have us believe. On this journey through the shadow of death I have been grateful beyond words for the amazing team of doctors, specialist nurses, ward staff (particularly on D3, where I have spent much of my inpatient time), housekeepers, cleaners and caterers who have cared for me during my ongoing treatment. I've felt the support of courageous and compassionate fellow patients.

One day, in a break from working on this chapter, as I was pacing back and forth along the ward corridor, I bumped into Sandy. Our paths had come together earlier on another ward. She remembered me. Now she was dying. Symptoms of the aggressive cancer that was rampaging through her lungs and beyond, and could not be treated further, had made her aware that she didn't want to fight any longer, that now was the time to be allowed to die peacefully, surrounded by her loved ones. She was not dramatic about the situation, but quietly accepting. The conversation we had warmed my heart and encouraged me onwards.

I'm conscious, too, of my beloved family and friends who have carried me through this process, each with different ways of offering support. More widely, I recognise people in every community who dare to live positive, generous lives that make life better for those around them. The men and women who choose to live (and die) positively are the people whose stories I want to inspire my own future, not the daily diet of tragic or inhumane stories that leave me feeling little hope for humanity. They help me to know that whatever the limitations of being human, we can change the world, or at least our small part of it, for the better.

Being agents of positive change requires a radical shift in the thinking of many of us. I recognise there are elements in our lives we cannot change: our genetic inheritance, the place and time of our birth, the family we are born into, the experiences we have when we are children and dependent on others, the unforeseen traumas that may happen to us. If any of these elements fall short of what might be considered a good start in life or a fortunate existence, this may affect the choices we make. Yet change still remains possible. What prevents it is not that it is impossible but that we believe it is not possible; or we prefer to stick with the narrative we have, rather than change the storyline, even if it's a destructive one.

Leadership trainers Alexander Grashow, Ronald Heifetz and Marty Linsky suggest that what 'people resist is not change per se, but loss'.[7] Unless we are deeply wounded by life we welcome positive change with open arms. If we are able to recognise what we may lose in a process of change – our sense of security or identity, finance, friendships, or whatever – we are in a better position to determine whether the loss might ultimately be outweighed by the gain, or to consider what emotional resources we may need to

accommodate an unavoidable loss. There is always a sense of insecurity, and often an impact on identity, when significant change
happens, when we alter the direction our stories have been taking.
Even positive changes, like getting married or going into a new job,
can destabilise us for a while or involve losses even as they provide
gains. By going into new 'territory' we have the chance to learn so
much more about ourselves, and to deepen our understanding of
life. Worthwhile change may be costly – a point I will return to
in Chapter 8. For now I want to look a little more closely at what
it means to exist.

7

To be or not to be . . .

Nine days after one of my chemotherapies I got up as usual at 5:30 a.m. to get a drink. I made it downstairs but once I was in the kitchen I found I could not stand up without beginning to faint. I waited for the symptoms to pass, but they didn't. I crawled into the lounge and onto the sofa, then rang my sister, Pat, who was asleep in the guest room. I asked her to wake Chris. Chris wouldn't hear the landline, and I could see his mobile on the coffee table. My temperature was just on the borderline that required me to ring the emergency cancer line. Keeping still, the dizziness eased, but when I checked my temperature an hour later it had gone up. On the advice of the nurse manning the emergency line I went to my local casualty department. Within an hour I felt really unwell. I was in isolation and on intravenous antibiotics. Later, I was transferred to the larger hospital where most of my care happened. I had neutropenic sepsis again.

When Mairéad first warned me about this possible complication I had asked if there was anything I could do to help myself or the team if it happened. Mairéad's reply was short, 'Exist.' Yet again she was right. As blood transfusions, intravenous antibiotics and drip fluids were given to me, I lay inert, sleeping or conscious but unmoving. Every so often I staggered the few feet to the toilet, wondering how the half-marathon runner I had been under a year ago could find walking the couple of metres to the loo so exhausting.

The words 'exist' or 'existence' come from the Latin *ex* (forth) and *sistere* (cause to stand), meaning 'to step out, stand forth, emerge, appear'. The experiences of this gap year made me think a great deal about what it means to exist, to stand forth in this extraordinary experience we call life.

Between my seventh and eighth chemotherapy sessions Chris and I visited a favourite spot on the coast close to where we live. It was a beautiful day. I could feel the sun on my face and the wind caressing the bristles on my head. I felt alive and well. We walked along the beach until we came to a D-Day memorial and the remains of slipways and other structures that had been built during the preparations for that day. We sat looking out to sea, each lost in our own thoughts. Eventually I asked Chris what he was thinking.

The D-Day ruins had reminded him of the story of a German bomber pilot in August 1940 who, having lost his bearings, dropped his bombs on residential London streets instead of the industrial and military targets planned. At that time Hitler had ordered his air force not to target civilians. As a result of the plane's bombs hitting London, Churchill ordered the RAF to bomb Berlin. In retaliation Hitler redirected his squadrons to blitz London. This change in his focus gave the RAF time to recover and regroup, and changed the course of the war.

The German pilot's error led to consequences he could never have imagined. It makes me think how so much of life experience is shaped as much by what we didn't intend, by our mistakes, as well as by our carefully laid plans. I can see how one small action or event can trigger consequences that further down the line have major ramifications. On the odd occasions during this illness when I'm not thinking very helpfully, I wonder what the actions and reactions were through my life that may over time have contributed to the changes in my body that led to my getting what one of my consultants called 'the rarest of rare cancers'. It's a pointless line of enquiry because this is the disease I'm dealing with now, and the past cannot be changed, even if I knew what, if anything, I could have changed.

All this made me think also of evolutionary theory, of how small changes over time have led to such extraordinary diversity of species, completely beyond the awareness of all the living things that were part of that process of change, until, that is, the most recent history of humankind. Existence unfolding! Today we have the capacity to determine whether or not the Earth will be a planet which continues to sustain life, or whether we will destroy ourselves and other species as a result of our stupidity and arrogance. As Lord Rees, the Astronomer Royal, writes,

> The Earth has existed for 45 million centuries, but this is the first when one species – ours – is so empowered that it can determine the planet's future . . . it is the first century where our follies could foreclose the immense potential for further evolution.[1]

This potential to bring to nothing all that has been, in earthly terms, tied in with some of my own thoughts while Chris was pondering the story of the German bomber. I was trying to get my head around Sartre's philosophy regarding the existence of nothing. This is not normally something I'd be thinking about, but when I mentioned to my dear friends Alison and Andrew that one of the chapters I was about to work on concerned existence, Andrew suggested I read Sartre's *Being and Nothingness*. Knowing nothing about Sartre, and following my commitment to read anything any friends suggested to me during this gap year, I did a bit of research about him.

Mindful that a little bit of knowledge can be very misleading I am not speaking now with any authority about Sartre's philosophy. I'm writing simply about how I understood what I read, and the thinking it triggered in me. Like any field of study, philosophy has its own shorthand language, which makes it pretty hard to get to grips with if, like me, you don't have a grasp of the terminology, but as I grappled with Sartre's ideas I was particularly struck by his thinking about nothingness. For Sartre, we come into existence, and then we create our essence through conscious choices. Through consciousness we also become aware of the existence of nothingness (no-thingness). This is more than abstract ideas of nothingness. We experience it. For example, a person who becomes blind during their life experiences the absence of sight, which shapes his experience of the world. The thing that is not sight. There are all kinds of absences which we experience. No-thingness is part of life. If I've understood Sartre, in order to recognise no-thingness, we have to be able to recognise the thing that is no longer present. A person who has been blind from birth will not have had the experience of sight being absent because, for them, it never existed in the first place. We only know that blindness exists because we know what it is to see.

Sitting by the sea with Chris, Sartre's thoughts about the existence of nothingness, and how the absence of 'things' (objects, people, experiences) shapes our lives, got me thinking about God and claims that God does or does not exist, and how, if at all, that affects my experience of living in the shadow of death. If, as Sartre suggests, we have to know the presence of something before we can recognise its absence, there's a problem when it comes to God: by definition, according to all the major world religions, God is the reality beyond human understanding. Therefore, if we can't recognise what is symbolised by the word 'God' we cannot say whether or not that ultimate reality exists.

Given this, what we end up doing is saying whether or not we buy into the different images of God human beings have created. When people tell me they don't believe in God, I always ask them what they mean by the word 'God'. More often than not, when they've described what they don't believe in, I say I don't believe in that description of God either, usually because it's a very inadequate, human-imagined picture of God.

Nor do I believe any more, some of the things people of faith claim is the activity of God. A devout Christian once told me that she and her husband had been arguing about what wallpaper to put in a particular room in their home. They prayed about it and lo, God led them to wallpaper they both loved. She gave it as an example of how God loved them and took care of them. I find it an utterly inadequate, even obscene, human image of God: one who sorts out this couple's wallpaper but ignores the millions praying to be saved from starvation or disease. Not that our images can be anything other than human creations, given that God is beyond our understanding. Yet, religious practitioners over time, in their arrogance and desire for power, have claimed to have the truth about God, to know what they cannot know, and to believe that anyone who doesn't accept this 'truth' is doomed and damned.

Throughout human history we see how inadequate beliefs about 'God', when combined with power struggles, have caused violent conflict and deep human pain. I say this as someone who once believed I had a hotline to God – in reality a rather larger version of my father – and who believed anyone who did not believe as I believed did not have the Truth. It has been a long journey to my present position of accepting that the word 'God' indicates a reality beyond my understanding. As St Paul made clear, 'For now we see in a mirror, dimly'.[2] In other words, we look to see God, but more often than not see only our own reflected images.

While I am in agreement with people of faith and atheists who reject clearly inadequate pictures of ultimate reality, I also question the dogmatism of atheists who believe they can know all there is to know about existence to the extent that they deny the word 'God' has any validity, as though they know everything. I think there is wisdom in theists and atheists alike holding what Chris calls a 'positive agnosticism'. I think there are ways of knowing that are other than my rational processes can define. I feel a deep connection with life, of being permeated and held by it, that goes beyond the love and care I have experienced from my medical team, family and friends. I can't, and don't want to, explain it as some kind of fact that can be pinned down. That feels inadequate. I know I have experienced it. I value very much those who try through poetic word or image to utter in some way their under-standing of that which is beyond understanding, or articulate the desire I know for myself, to keep seeking that which is so elusive.

I know that there is more to the cosmos, from the sub-atomic to the vastness of space, than I can ever comprehend. I do not see the wisdom inherent in aspects of religious tradition as being at odds with the discoveries and unfolding understanding of science. I think that within religious traditions, particularly when their expressions take non-literal forms, there is much that connects with science. Before saying more about that, I want to note how living in the shadow of death has influenced my thoughts about God and God-talk.

As I was coming towards the end of the planned treatment, Andrew, a friend and colleague, sent me an invitation to a small colloquium on the interface between the sacred and secular, and how facilitators and mediators work across the divide. As I thought about the theme I realised that I no longer see reality in terms of a sharp divide between sacred and secular. There is simply life in all its creative and destructive complexity. We have created these potential ghettoes of sacred and secular according to whether or not we think there is a 'more than' to life that is beyond comprehension, and to whether or not we want to be part of humankind's corporate attempts to give shape to that ultimate reality. In this place of life-threatening illness, the religious affiliation or otherwise of those around me, my medical team, the nurses, and the patients with whom I'm sharing the journey of living and dying with cancer, is irrelevant. What matters is the care and compassion with which they treat me, in other words, the humanity of their actions. This perception tallies with the experience of others in dire circumstances. To the hungry it is the food offered, not the faith of the giver that is of greatest import. The Jesus of the Gospel of Matthew indicates it is not those who believe the 'right' things, but who do the right things – feed the hungry, give shelter to the homeless, visit the imprisoned, clothe the naked – who access the kingdom of heaven, a reality in the here and now, not a life-after-death experience.

It strikes me that very quickly the developing church lost sight of the primacy of right ways of living (orthopraxis), and became preoccupied with right ways of believing (orthodoxy). The compulsion to make sure people believed the right things – that is, what the dominant church view was at the time – led organised religion to terribly inhumane actions at times. And so it continues today across the major world faiths. This is not to deny that there are individual people and communities of faith who have carried out, and continue to carry out, deeply humanitarian and heroic work, but it is only part of the picture. Perhaps what the world needs today are people of all faiths and none, who sit lightly to the differing sacred or secular labels we've created but are committed to working together to heal the wounds of our world, at a human level and environmentally. Maybe this task is about learning to hallow *all* of life, to honour it as holy, rather than to take it for granted or abuse it.

At present, we have leaders who seem to be leading us in the direction of war or the destruction of our environment, the outcomes of which can only be deadly for humankind, yet far too few voices across the nations are agitating for change and saying our present behaviours are not the way forward. Most of us are getting on with our lives, perhaps expressing our concern, but not doing anything about adding to the pressure for change, perhaps because change may demand something of us that we are not willing to give. It's as though we take life for granted. Yet should those few in power determine the future of the rest of us? We are not powerless, though perhaps, in the face of profound challenges, it feels easier to say we are helpless, and to abdicate the responsibility we all have to make life better for all people.

I think there is a particular challenge to people of faith. Our scriptures and traditions hold wisdom that is true for all times and places alongside beliefs that were the attempts of people in one time and place to make the human–divine connection, but which no longer hold true because of what we have subsequently learnt about life. Once, I understood the Bible to be literally true, but studying it over the years and allowing a conversation between scripture and my experience revealed to me that to hold it as literally true is to limit, not liberate, its power. The Gospels are in my blood, but while I think they contain history to some degree, I think they also convey truth through the storytelling of those inspired by the person of Jesus, and, consciously and unconsciously, the writers have conveyed not only history but your story and my story. I value the key stories of the Gospels, from the Virgin birth to the Resurrection, not because I think some of these things happened in one time and place, but because I experience them happening in my story and the stories of the people I meet and work with. Where I most experience them is in the compassionate humanity of men and women from all walks of life, some of whom would be regarded as 'not saved' by some of my fellow Christians, precisely because they're perceived as not believing the right things.

In the Hebrew scriptures, the great prophet Elijah is so bound by the old ways of seeing God in earthquake, wind and fire, that when God does not reveal Godself through these elements but in the sound of sheer silence, Elijah doesn't recognise it. I think the church in some of its expressions is a modern Elijah, deaf to what it needs to hear today, and blind to the divine because the glimpses we may have of ultimate reality are not coming in a form recognisable to particular belief patterns. But this is not just a challenge to people of faith.

All of us, regardless of our faith or lack of it, are capable of holding to beliefs and behaviours that keep us in our comfort zone, that make us blind or deaf, and which we're reluctant to relinquish when new understanding challenges our position. I suggest there is an Elijah voice in every one of us that reiterates the same old, same old, because we're too fearful or lazy or ignorant or convinced of our rightness to entertain the possibility that there may be other ways of understanding that may be helpful or a more accurate expression of reality.

For me this time of illness has been an unwanted but wonderful opportunity to re-evaluate my life and understanding, to determine what's important, what may be learnt from the past, lived fully in the present, and taken forward into whatever future I may have left. I have been sustained through this time by family and friends, many, but not all of whom are steeped in faith traditions of one kind or another. Of the many, all are well aware of the limitations of organised religion. Everyone has responded to me with love and compassion. Words of encouragement and support have been the priority. They have met me where I am psychologically. They have shared poetry, visual images, empathetic silence, stories, books, academic papers and only very occasionally texts from scripture, as they have been responsive to our conversations. They have made me laugh and held me when I've cried (in reality or with virtual hugs).

On the rare times I have been out of hospital on Sundays, I have found restoration in the silence of Quaker meetings. I have been inspired as well by the choral music in the cathedral, sitting behind the choir for Evensong, but I found the Anglican liturgy in which I've been rooted since childhood far too wordy and failing to give expression to the faith that remains so vital to me. The sermons I've heard have felt irrelevant to where I am now, and the content of some has seemed more fitting for six-year-olds than intelligent adults. I'm sure there are churches I could go to where this is not the case, but I no longer feel the need for church in the way I once did. I have found my own community of people who support and affirm me, challenge and inspire me, ask me awkward questions when they need asking, and share this journey of life with openness and curiosity. While my need to be part of organised religion has diminished, my pilgrimage of faith remains as important to me as it ever was, because every life is an act of faith. We can't avoid uncertainty or heartbreak if we choose to live and love fully. The question is, what is our motivation for existence?

In *A Place of Greater Safety*, Hilary Mantel's novel about the French Revolution, Georges-Jacques visits his sister, a nun. She asks him what he wants out of life. He replies, 'I suppose it means I want to get a position, to have money, to make people respect me . . . I just want to be somebody.'[3] Although money has never been a motivating factor for me, except to earn enough to pay my bills, I can identify with Georges-Jacques' desire to be somebody.

But I think life is about so much more than 'being somebody'. That's just as well, since illness seemingly limits my potential to be somebody in conventional terms – to be renowned through my actions, to be a dynamic force for good. It has turned upside-down my sense of self and where my worth lies. What exactly my life will be if I live beyond treatment, I cannot picture. All I know is that it will be different as a result of this living with cancer. This is not just because I've been living in the shadow of death in a very obvious way, but because the gift of this disease has been time to reflect on life, knowing I may lose it.

Confronted by the possibility that I may die sooner than expected concentrates the mind on questions of meaning, and how I interpret my present experience in the context of wider and ultimate reality. While I criticised earlier the kind of belief that spoke of God sorting out minor issues in our lives while leaving millions to die of starvation and disease, I am conscious of having experiences that appear to have a significance which goes beyond what anyone might define simply as random events. Jung referred to these experiences as part of the collective unconscious, and he noted the sense of synchronicity we have when they happen. For me, this awareness of a force or energy at work within and beyond me is not the anthropomorphic image of God familiar to many people of faith. I find resonances with it in quantum physics.

Referring to quantum physics in her paper on 'Spirit and Matter', analytical psychotherapist Melanie Gibson writes about 'active information'.[4] I didn't know what this was so I did some research. Even before I became ill I struggled to get my head around quantum physics. 'Chemo brain' – the feeling while undergoing chemotherapy that I'm thinking through a thick layer of cotton wool – makes understanding all the more difficult. I don't want to give the false impression that I understood much of what I read. What captured my imagination was that for many physicists,

'Matter is merely bound energy and can be returned to energy. The universe should be viewed not as a collection of things but as a series of interacting processes.'[5] I was struck by the similarity of the language to that in a quote from Teilhard de Chardin that Melanie uses in her paper, 'Matter is spirit moving slowly enough to be seen.' I love this perspective. It suggests there is energy/spirit that under the influence of different forces or processes can take different forms, such as matter.

I am exasperated by my incapacity to grasp and articulate competently the significance of quantum physics. What I intuit from reading Melanie's paper is that the dualistic view of body and spirit I explored and rejected in Chapter 5 ('Who am I?') is also rejected by present-day scientific theories such as quantum physics. As we observe, the energy of the expanding cosmos is hard to comprehend. Explosions of energy that destroy whatever lies in their wake may be part of creative processes. Destruction and creation need not necessarily be opposed forces but different aspects of the constant transformation of energy. At a human level we see humankind channelling the energy of life creatively and destructively. Religious traditions speak of this energy as spirit, a dimension of ultimate reality, a force for ultimate good. Like the wind, it blows where it wills, uncontainable and uncontrollable. In religious language the spirit at work in humankind is a power that transforms lives and motivates those who are aware of and open to its 'current', to living love, compassion, justice, mercy, hospitality, leadership and every other way of being we have traditionally attributed to the Being of God. Religious discipline is about trying to align ourselves with this energy, getting into its wind-stream, if you like, adding to the common good and creating positive energy ourselves. The more we are at one within our own psyches, with each other and with our environment, the greater our potential to live out this life force that is the essence of everything.

I've felt more closely this connection since I've been ill, although I have experienced it at other key times in my life. I do not think of the energy I'm describing in terms of it being sacred or secular. I think the energy of life cannot be compartmentalised. It can only be lived into and lived out as we adjust the sails of experience to feel its force more fully. Experiences of abuse and deprivation caused by the absence of love may lead us to feel 'out of kilter' with life and alienated from others. In response we in turn may use the energy of life as a force to cause harm, rather than a source of healing.

Most of the time, I suspect, we are unaware of this energy at our core, this spirit that is part of life. How can people struggling simply to survive feel its force? In our own supposedly civilised society the have-nots increasingly struggle to get by. Increasing numbers of people seem to echo the sentiments expressed by Lucille Duplessis in her diary entry of 6 June 1789 in Hilary Mantel's *A Place of Greater Safety*:

Must we crawl forever? When shall we find the happiness we seek? Man is easily dazzled . . . when he forgets himself he thinks he is happy. No, there is no happiness on earth, it is only a chimera.[6]

While I was thinking about this chapter a newspaper article reminded me that men under the age of forty-five are three times more likely than women to commit suicide. I wonder about the society we have created in which significant groups of people feel so alienated that non-existence is preferable to the lives they have. I think too, of the living deaths we accept in our world. During my year of treatment in 2017 I noted the man-made cholera epidemic in Yemen and the poverty and disease in many parts of the world that could be alleviated if more of us sought to make that a reality by challenging the corrupt political systems, the big businesses and the sheer inhumanity that causes people to suffer. This is not to deny the amazing individuals and groups that are working for change, but it is not enough.

The happiness Lucille Duplessis describes as an illusion intrigues me. The energy of existence is about much more than happiness, but happiness may be one outcome of how we channel that energy. What is happiness? In more recent years there have been books and projects specifically focused on happiness, a point which suggests they have been motivated by the awareness that happiness is in short supply. I realised as I began to think more about happiness that I couldn't easily define it. The word is rooted in 'hap', the Norwegian/Viking word meaning luck, suggesting happiness is not a given for life, but very much the result of chance. I started asking those around me what happiness was for them. They spoke about feelings of contentment, warmth, fulfilment, peace, pleasure, energy or purpose. Some spoke of needs being met making them happy. For one friend, happiness is a full fridge because as a child he knew hunger. This challenges the idea that you can't make happiness happen, although in my experience happiness usually comes as a by-product of something else.

My own sense of what happiness is has changed through my illness. I have always understood myself to be a restless soul, driven to achieve, although I haven't been certain exactly what it is I have needed to achieve. Happiness came through fulfilling and success-ful work or through a deep sense of connectedness in relationships with those I love. It was dependent on external factors being right. Illness has taught me that happiness is about what's going on inside me, not what's happening on the outside. For those looking on, my present situation is terrible – and make no mistake, some of it has been grim beyond words – yet I have experienced a degree of contentment, a sense of peace, and immense gratitude during this illness that previously eluded me. I have relinquished some of the drivenness and come to an acceptance of myself and of the uncertainty of life that, for the most part, has enabled me to sit more easily with who I am and what has happened to me as I've travelled through the valley of the shadow of death. I have known moments of freedom and joy.

I do not take these unexpected outcomes lightly. I wonder if they are fleeting, and whether I can sustain the internal 'at-oneness' when I am engaging with wider life after treatment. Through treatment I have had a very clear focus to enable my medical team to do all they need to do without making their task more difficult, to attend to the questions and challenges that have arisen, and, in so far as I am able, to navigate this time with grace, calm and gratitude. With treatment has come hope – the hope of cure. When treatment ends the landscape will be one of uncertainty and, should the cancer return, there is unlikely to be further treatment offering remission, since I have had the most intensive treatment possible. I notice a shift in my emotions as I approach the final month in isolation (more of that in the next chapter), a disquiet.

All of this reminds me how, as I've considered normal life from the shadow of death, far too many of us are existing rather than living; accepting a life that at the very least feeds into our inner despair and causes us to question whether it's worth it. If this chapter asks nothing else, it is for each of us to wake up, to be attentive, to take time to notice the extraordinary nature of being, in all its complexity, and to answer the question posed by Mary Oliver at the end of her poem, 'The Summer Day':

> Tell me, what is it you plan to do
> with your one wild and precious life?[7]

8

Hitting the depths

Throughout my stay in hospital I was extremely grateful for the League of Friends' volunteers, who trundled their newspaper and sweets trolley around the wards so that those of us too incapacitated to wander down to the shops in the hospital foyer could still keep up with national and international events, as well as pass the time with the puzzle pages. If I missed the moment they passed by because I was in the bathroom or isolated in a side room they couldn't access, I felt quite bereft. In November 2017 I noted a report about a study of cancer patients which concluded that the stress of discovering they have cancer leads one in five people to develop post-traumatic stress disorder (PTSD).[1] This was not my experience. I think that, for the most part, I have felt calm and positive. Until the final month in the Isolation Unit, that is.

Right from our early meetings Mairéad said that when a person comes out of the month in isolation that completes their planned treatment, many suffer from post-traumatic stress symptoms and feel completely disorientated. Earlier in the year I found this difficult to believe. After three chemotherapies put me into neutropenic sepsis I knew what it was to feel awful for a while, but

I also seemed to bounce back quite quickly once I received the necessary inpatient treatment. I assumed, wrongly as it turns out, that the final month would be a similar experience.

I was keen for it to get underway. It was a key part of the treatment and increased the possibility that I might be cured. Already I was beginning to think about post-treatment recovery and how I might begin to re-engage with wider life. After everything I had learnt about the importance of living in the moment, I was still thinking about the future, despite not being in any position to make useful decisions about it. Sometimes the lessons we need to learn are clear, yet putting them into practice proves a constant challenge. I was painfully reminded of my stupidity in this respect when complications occurred as I was preparing for the isolation month.

Chris and I were walking by the sea a few days after my last four-day chemotherapy. I had been feeling really well, but not long after arriving at the coast nausea began to kick in and my abdomen felt distended and uncomfortable. As we walked I began to feel worse. We sat on a sheltered bench and my mouth kept filling with pre-vomiting fluid, but the vomit wouldn't come. Finally it emerged when I was back in the car, then again on the journey home, then two litres of it once we got home. Lying on the sofa with a hot water bottle on my abdomen I felt easier. By the morning I was better and, with the encouragement of one of my consultants, we went off to Dorset for a few days' break before I was to be admitted to the Isolation Unit. I walked along the cliff paths, visited castles and stately homes, ate and drank well. I felt almost normal.

On our way home we called in to Stourhead, a National Trust property. We were walking around the grounds when I was doubled up suddenly with acute abdominal pain and the world began to spin. I sat for a while bent over, waiting for the dizziness and pain to ease. After a while I started to walk back to the car but the pain escalated again after a few paces, and I was sick. Much to my embarrassment a buggy had to be called to come and pick me up and return us to the car park. From there we had an hour's drive home. The pain came in waves. I tried not to cry out and distract Chris from driving. As we neared our local hospital I rang the emergency oncology line and was advised to go straight to Casualty. I ended up in hospital for a week with questions about whether surgery was needed and whether the inflammation was anything more sinister than an infection in my intestine around the earlier surgery site. Thankfully, I responded well to intravenous antibiotics and once all my blood levels were back to normal I was able to go home.

It was a salutary reminder that no matter how well I felt, my guts were vulnerable. I am this body but so much goes on within me, for good and ill, over which I have no conscious control. This disease has left parts of me physically fragile regardless of how strong I feel mentally. I have needed to relearn what my capacities and limitations are, and whether they are temporary or permanent. Back to taking one day at a time and leaving the future to take care of itself!

The most disturbing aspect of the infection was that my emergency admission clashed with my admission date for the final month in isolation and the latter had to be put on hold. I felt very unsettled. While my team had prepared me all along the way for the various complications that were likely to happen and, as a result, when they occurred, I was able to take them in my stride, the abdominal pain and infection had come out of the blue and delayed the final and vital part of my treatment. It threw me.

Once I was cleared to go ahead with it I then had to wait for another bed to become available in the Isolation Unit. Possible days came and went. It was a time again of uncertainty and waiting, with the need to be prepared to go in at short notice. I was grateful to staff who thought to let me know if a potential bed on a certain day didn't work out. I had to remind myself constantly to live only in the present moment, not to fret about the delay or be unsettled by the uncertainty and, while I was waiting, to do something constructive to keep me focused in the here and now.

When the phone call came unexpectedly saying a bed was ready for me later that day, it was not only good news but information again requiring mental adjustment. The fact that it was happening at last brought home not only its potential to rid me fully of the lymphoma, but also the life-threatening risks of the treatment. Should I tell key people in my life how much I love them just in case I didn't survive the next month? I didn't want to be over-dramatic, and I had weathered all the treatment and complications to date pretty well. Yet there was a greater risk with this part of the treatment and I didn't want to die not having left my loved ones with final words of how much they mean to me.

It was October and the season of mellow, melancholic autumn as I pondered these things. The tree canopy along the road to the hospital was aflame with reds, oranges, yellows and burnished gold as the leaves died gloriously before falling to the ground. The nights were drawing in rapidly. The mornings were damp and misty. The season reflected my mood. Just before I went into isolation my friend, Sue, sent me W.B. Yeats' poem, 'The Wild Swans at Coole'.[2] It tells of the poet repeating his annual count of a bank of swans taking off in the half-light of an October evening. For nineteen years he has observed this spectacle, and seems to have found its pattern reassuring. This time, though, he is struck by just how much has changed since he first counted the swans all those years ago, and there's a real sense of loss in his words.

I have loved this poem for a long time. I imagined the wild beauty of swans climbing the sky would sustain me during the time in isolation. Like Yeats, I knew, also, that 'All's changed'. My sense of physical invincibility was gone. The 'wild swans' of my being were grounded, and I didn't know for how long! Driving to hospital for admission to the Isolation Unit I felt on edge.

Once settled in my room in the unit I settled emotionally as well, at least on that first day. I was back in the small, contained world of illness, and 'normal' life was elsewhere. This I could deal with. The task for the following few weeks was basic: to keep myself as fit as possible, to ride as lightly as possible through the expected chemo complications, and to make sure I did everything I could to enable my team to do what they needed to do. The future was on hold, at least in terms of me having to sort it out.

The next day I was given the chemotherapy drug Carmustine. My nurse told me that it was a component of mustard gas and came to medical attention in the First World War when the victims of gas attack showed symptoms of bone marrow suppression. Now it was being infused into me to wipe out my bone marrow and any remaining lymphoma cells. It was given intravenously in alcohol of some kind. I quickly experienced the hot flush expected, and nausea was triggered. By the end of the day I had a throbbing headache, an aching throat and prickly mouth and lips. I hadn't reacted quite so immediately to previous chemos, apart from putting on kilos of fluid and becoming the Michelin woman with the methotrexate infusions. I wasn't expecting the reaction to this chemo so, as I lay awake through much of the night feeling rough, I wondered about my capacity to weather this treatment. Luckily by morning I felt better and Mairéad assured me such side effects were 'normal'.

After I told my lovely sister-in-law, Jan, about the Carmustine, she, like me, was struck by how a weapon of war had eventually become an agent of healing. It reminded her of the biblical story of Joseph and words he speaks to his brothers who sold him into slavery in Egypt, but with whom he later reconciles. Of their actions he says, 'Even though you intended to do harm to me, God intended it for good . . .'[3] So much of what exists in our world either can be used to destroy, or to build up human life. The question is, how will we humans choose to use the bounty of the Earth? More importantly, Carmustine and its history remind me that out of death-dealing situations, something life-giving can emerge if we put our hearts and minds to it. This Carmustine story speaks of hope, a subject I shall return to in the next chapter, but first I want to talk about more painful reality.

Three days into the five days of chemotherapy I developed diarrhoea. It turned out to be norovirus. I do not have the words to express how obliterated I felt as a person, how ill I was, and how everything that helped me know myself was stripped away by the isolation chemo and the norovirus. Within a few short days I ceased to be able to use my own toilet and sometimes needed help simply to get onto the commode that became a fixture by my bed. As much as every hour, and sometimes more, day and night, I was out on the commode pouring out liquid instead of solid. No treatment could be given because the only way to get rid of the virus was to excrete it.

Norovirus caused the side-effects of the chemotherapy to kick in earlier. I had no immunity by now. Various combinations of intravenous antibiotics were given to treat my high temperatures. I all but ceased eating, and it was impossible to drink enough to replace what I was losing. My mouth was constantly so dry that my tongue stuck to the roof of my mouth. 'Salvation' came in the form of ice pops. I could lie in bed sucking on the sticks of flavoured ice and for a short time feel my mouth refreshed. I could lie flat and crunch on the ice and it would go down slowly so I didn't choke. I marvel still how something so inconsequential should have been the source of such comfort in that dark time.

My taste buds were affected by the chemo so food and drinks I normally liked tasted awful, and my mouth, throat, gullet and guts were sore. Neutropenic sepsis set in as expected. A combination of morphine and anti-emetic caused me to lose track of some periods of time: people appeared and disappeared at the end of my bed. Sometimes I would be talking to someone but on opening my eyes find the room empty. For days Chris sat by me, holding my hand while I lay silent and inert. I could not have got through without him. My two chest lines, and another cannula in my arm fed in fluid, electrolytes, antibiotics and blood transfusions. I simply existed. The word 'God' felt meaningless. The phrase 'God is love' meant nothing, except through the human touch of those who cared for me during that time.

For almost a month my only outlook was the walls of the hospital outside my window. I was starved of beauty to the degree that as the diarrhoea began to subside I felt desperate to leave isolation. For weeks I hadn't had the strength or will to look at messages on my phone so I'd missed the photos of lovely places friends had sent. My brain was incapable of much thought. My overwhelming feelings were of vulnerability and the fear that I might never be able to do again the work I had done before becoming ill.

I do not think I am unusual as a human being to need beauty in my life, to feel inspired by the creativity of artists as well as being sustained by the natural beauty of the Earth. Looking around our cities I notice how architects have sometimes condemned people to live in brutal housing estates and confined spaces, forgetting how much the human spirit requires visually lovely contexts in order to thrive. Today we need much more affordable housing, but does 'affordable' mean we must make people live in ugly, cramped contexts, in which no one would ever *choose* to live?

As I began to 'come to' and to struggle more with the soulless, bland space in which I had to stay I realised how traumatic the month was being for me. I had lost my capacity to respond positively. I wasn't even enduring what was happening. Endurance might suggest I was willing myself to get through. In reality I carried on because there was no other option. Whether I lived or died depended on the team's capacity to get my blood and my body back in balance. Apart from keeping on keeping on, I felt useless in the process. The stem cell transplant I had immediately the chemotherapy ended began to give me neutrophils again, but deep in the core of my being grief was beginning to bubble up. This treatment might offer me the best chance of cure but it was necessarily toxic, and felt destructive to my body. As I began to recover, a friend spoke about how I was through the worst, and could now look forward to better times rather than dwelling on what I'd just been through. It was an understandable reaction but one that felt utterly wrong to me.

Emerging out of the month in the Isolation Unit I knew this experience was not one to be moved on from at speed just because it was now past. I understand from my work with individuals and communities coming out of conflict or dealing with profound trauma that there are experiences of such significance that happen to us as individuals or communities that we need to mark them in some way, to say in something more than words, 'This happened to me and impacts greatly on who I am'. That month in the Isolation Unit was such an experience for me.

While thinking about this chapter as I began to recover in the Isolation Unit, I watched the Remembrance Sunday service from the Cenotaph and registered the people for whom the remembering of what happened remains crucial to their identity and sense of well-being. The wounds of their war experience continue to find healing in the remembering. Somehow, through the remembering, shattered selves begin to piece themselves back together, to re-establish their identity and place in the scheme of things. This isn't a quick fix, but it is crucial to human well-being.

In much more recent times we have watched men, women and children make epic journeys as refugees, often profoundly traumatic and completely life-changing flights from the destruction of war, terrorism or unbearable deprivation. They arrive in the UK and become part of communities that have no comprehension of what they've been through, and often no sense that before people can integrate into a new life, they need to be able to process what has happened to them. They need to tell their stories, create way-markers and memorials that affirm the immensity of what they've experienced. Dismissed as 'collateral damage', they need to be able to stand tall again as human beings who know themselves worthy of acknowledgement and respect. Organisations like the Medical Foundation for the Care of Victims of Torture help new arrivals to work with the trauma they've survived, but I'm conscious of another dynamic at work: the desire to brush under the carpet anything that disturbs our sense of well-being and reminds us that life is more precarious than we want to admit. We've watched the devastation of hurricanes in the Caribbean, and the shocked people not knowing where to begin the clear-up, and I wonder what space has been or will be made over coming months for those people simply to sit with what has happened to them, to acknowledge the destruction and loss they have witnessed.

We live life at such speed today that we do not always process what we need to address in our experience that has impacted profoundly upon us. I knew that before I could move on well from what I thought was the last month of treatment, I must 'sit with' its impact upon me. I knew I needed to grieve, and to acknowledge the degree of physical impairment and mental shut-down that I felt. I needed to do this in order to deal with the trauma of that time, and to lay to rest its legacy of grief. I needed to be able to say how bloody the experience was, and to have that heard, so that I could move on to acknowledge fully the great skill of my team in getting me through and providing a treatment which, devastating as it was, offered me the chance of cure.

Without the time to work with our significant experiences, we end up carrying them as unhealed wounds. We may never feel heard, and life goes on around us but we're never fully part of it. Fear and panic may suddenly overwhelm us out of the blue. Tiredness and insomnia, nightmares and flashbacks may pepper our days and nights. Depression and other symptoms of mental ill-health may limit our capacity to live fully. The key to the kind of remembering I think is essential is that we remember in order to be re-membered, that is, made whole. We do not remember in order to remain in a place of anguish and fragmentation, but so that we may stand tall again. There's a story in the Gospels about a woman who has been bleeding for twelve years and is healed by Jesus. Her infirmity makes her an outcast, ritually impure as a result of the constant loss of blood. She lives in the shadows, fearful of attention: one more person who has fallen by the wayside of inhumanity. When Jesus is in the neighbourhood she slips through the crowd unnoticed, as always, and touches the fringe of his cloak. She has this mad idea that the touch will be enough to cure her, and indeed it is. Her aim is to slip away again without attention but,

> . . . Jesus asked, 'Who touched me?' When all denied it, Peter said, 'Master, the crowds surround you and press in on you.' But Jesus said, 'Someone touched me; for I noticed that power had gone out from me.' When the woman saw that she could not remain hidden, she came trembling; and falling down before him, she declared in the presence of all the people why she had touched him, and how she had been immediately healed. He said to her, 'Daughter, your faith has made you well; go in peace.'[4]

For so long the woman has been treated as a non-person. She thinks of herself in that way. When Jesus asks who touched him, the woman need not have disclosed her presence or actions for the very reasons Peter gives, but Jesus is offering her an important opportunity. It is an invitation to stand tall, to tell her story, to be heard, to know herself as a person whose actions impact on others, and, in return, to be affirmed for who she is, to be called a daughter, a beloved person of significance. The woman's conversation with Jesus acts as an emotional 'way-marker'. It marks an ending to living insignificantly, and heralds a new beginning.

When it comes to catastrophic human experiences, like those of genocide or war, human communities are generally good at telling their stories and erecting their wayside memorials in the aftermath. We are less good at recognising the importance of, or enabling such processes for traumatised individuals or communities whose pain we have not fully understood, particularly when it doesn't happen on quite the scale of international conflict. In part this may be because we find the pain of others difficult to live with. We may hold their pain at bay because we haven't addressed our own and theirs becomes too close for comfort. We may simply not recognise what another person has lived through because it is so outside the realms of our own experience. Taking time to listen, to hear without judging, and to mark significant events in the life of another person, helps in healing the wounds of our world and of one another.

For myself, I recognised my need to talk with one or two trusted friends about the month in isolation, to cry a bit more and, at some point during the following months, to use art, music, poetry or some kind of symbolic ritual to mark the experience so that I could move on without the raw emotions with which losing all sense of my self in the Isolation Unit left me.

9

Now what?

Leaving hospital from the Isolation Unit felt very daunting because I was so physically vulnerable. Any common infection that once I shrugged off with ease could now make me seriously unwell. The smallest amount of activity exhausted me. It was three days before I attempted to walk the ten minutes into Winchester and back. I was wiped out by that. Yet being able to leave the unit also meant I was entering a new realm: that of recovery. I was still a patient under the care of the team. I was a shadow of my former self. It was likely that I'd end up back in hospital with infections I couldn't fight, but gradually I needed to reintegrate back into the life I hoped to lead as a well person, or at least one with time to enjoy life for whatever length of it remained. This was the time that from the beginning of treatment I felt I would find hardest to navigate.

I had been ill and a patient for the whole year. Aspects of treatment had become so much a part of my life that on two occasions in hospital I walked my mobile IV fluid (drip) stand out to the loo with me, only to realise when I came back that, for once, I wasn't actually attached to a drip at that point. It made me, the women in the bay and the nurses laugh, but it also showed the extent to which I was on automatic pilot, getting through each day.

I began to feel disquiet about the post-treatment time after my last four-day chemo and before the final month in isolation. The sense of calm that had been with me for the most part to that point began to be interjected with moments of concern as I pondered what life might look like when the intensive treatment ended. I had to keep drawing my thinking back into the present, to stop trying to imagine what, from that point in time, was not imaginable in any helpful way. How could I know what I'd feel; what I'd be capable of, and when; what state I'd be in physically and whether I'd have much time to live? I needed to trust that things would become clear when that time came. Advance planning was a pointless exercise.

At the end of the treatment plan, when I'd been out of the Isolation Unit for almost two weeks and knew I was getting stronger each day, I stood, a little shell-shocked, looking across the River Styx, knowing I needed to make the return journey to 'normal' life, or at least the life I wanted to live. As I looked at the road ahead, I thought in a dazed way, 'Now what? . . . Aaaaah!' There's a poignant story in the Gospel of John that encapsulates well this experience. I want to emphasise that, for me, this story is not about a one-off physical healing, but a profound insight into the dynamics at work in all of us as we struggle to deal with the ways in which life experience sometimes paralyses our ability to go forward and keeps us stuck in unhealthy attitudes and behaviours. The man is part of my own psyche.

Now in Jerusalem by the Sheep Gate there is a pool, called in Hebrew Beth-zatha, which has five porticoes. In these lay many invalids – blind, lame, and paralysed. One man was there who had been ill for thirty-eight years. When Jesus saw him lying there and knew that he had been there a long time, he said to him, 'Do you want to be made well?' The sick man answered him, 'Sir, I have no one to put me into the pool when the water is stirred up; and while I am making my way, someone else steps down ahead of me.' Jesus said to him, 'Stand up, take your mat and walk.' At once the man was made well, and he took up his mat and began to walk . . . Later Jesus found him in the temple and said to him, 'See, you have been made well! Do not sin anymore, so that nothing worse happens to you.'[1]

'Do you want to be made well?' seems a ridiculous question to ask a sick person, but it couldn't be more astute and, as with many of the healing stories, the truth encapsulated is about much more than physical healing. The human dynamics at work in the paralysed man exist as much in those of us who consider ourselves fit and healthy as those of us who are very obviously ill.

The man in this story has been paralysed for thirty-eight years. He is part of the community of sick people by the pool. His world is small and he knows its ins and outs. In all probability he gets enough to eat from the alms-giving expected of the wider community. His life is limited and tough but it is familiar to him. It's interesting that when Jesus asks him if he wants to be healed, he doesn't answer the question with a straight 'Yes!' as one might expect, but tells Jesus that without help he can't get into the water quickly enough when it is stirred up by bubbles and pressure from the deeper springs sourcing the pool. Some believed that when this natural phenomenon happened, those first in the water would be healed: a view bearing some resemblance to the belief in more modern times that 'taking the water' and bathing in the springs of spa towns like Bath, Buxton and Harrogate promoted health and healing.

To me the man's words have the feel of an excuse being made by someone lacking in confidence, and content to stay put because the effort required for change feels beyond him. If he is enabled to stand on his own two feet he will no longer be part of this poolside community as he has been for so long. He will have to find employment to sustain himself since he won't be eligible any more for charitable help. He will need to develop a different identity from the one he has had all these years, moving from victim to survivor to healthy man. There is no guarantee that everything will work out. His known world may be hard, but the unknown life that healing will open up for him looks utterly terrifying from where he now lies. Once healed by Jesus it is not surprising that he goes and hides himself away in the temple until Jesus finds him and sends him on his way with firm words. I wonder if the 'sin' Jesus tells the man not to repeat is his fear of living a full and flourishing life, and his seeming preference to remain stuck where he is rather than move on.

As I reflected on my life at the end of treatment, the man's reactions were utterly understandable. I had only been fully out of action for eight months. By the time I expected to be considered fit enough to start working again at least a year would have passed since I had first become ill. I wondered if I would be able to build up my workload again, whether I was as competent as before I became ill, and whether my colleagues would all have moved on with their working lives, leaving me behind. Even if they hadn't, what work could I do, now the damage to my immune system meant that some of the international work I was developing was no longer possible? Behind this lack of confidence lay deeper questions about the length of time I might live, the priorities I wanted to embrace, and how I made the changes I had come to think important as I considered normal life from the shadow of death. So much around which to get my chemo-brained head!

I imagine the paralysed man would have taken great strengths into a life standing on his own two feet, because to survive as he had all those years was no mean achievement, but he would need a different mind-set for the new context. 'Mind-set' is at times a good way of describing our mental state. Over time our minds become set in certain patterns that are hard to change. When Marion Partington's sister disappeared it was twenty years before anyone learnt she had been a victim of the serial murderers Fred and Rosemary West. Working to come to terms with this discovery Marion notes:

> It has been hard for the habits of my unconscious to be free of the loops of two decades of Not Knowing. The mind gets into habits that need dissolving. The rat runs of my mind are no longer an appropriate response.[2]

Ways of thinking and behaving that work in one set of circumstances may fall short in other contexts, yet well-used thought patterns, like well-used paths, are easier to access than neglected neural pathways in our brain. To make use of them we need to be mindful of our default reactions and very consciously choose different attitudes until these become more naturally established and instinctive. This is true not only of individual mind-sets but also of communal consciousness. Sometimes, thankfully, enough individuals over time change their personal perspective to cause a shift in communal thinking. Sometimes new awareness from outside a community imposes change upon the members of that community. The process may be painful and provoke conflict, within or between ourselves, but it is essential if we are to live to our greatest creative potential and not annihilate ourselves.

For such change to happen we need hope, but what exactly is that? Is it anything more than wishful thinking, or is it rooted in something deeper? Until I first experienced despair, I thought of hope as a wonderful, life-giving gift. When profound loss caught up with me and I couldn't seem to get myself back on track, hope suddenly became a source of fear. If you believe in the light at the end of the tunnel and it doesn't come, despair is even harder to deal with than if you had not hoped in the first place. Maya Angelou captures the ultimate despair of this kind of hope in her poem, 'A Plagued Journey':

> There is no warning rattle at the door
> nor heavy feet to stomp the foyer boards.
> Safe in the dark prison, I know that
> light slides over
> the fingered work of a toothless
> woman in Pakistan.
> Happy prints of
> an invisible time are illumined.
> My mouth agape
> rejects the solid air and
> lungs hold. The invader takes
> direction and
> seeps through the plaster walls.
> It is at my chamber, entering
> the keyhole, pushing
> through the padding of the door.
> I cannot scream. A bone
> of fear clogs my throat.
> It is upon me. It is
> sunrise, with Hope
> its arrogant rider.
> My mind, formerly quiescent
> in its snug encasement, is strained

to look upon their rapturous visages,
to let them enter even into me.
I am forced
outside myself to
mount the light and ride joined with Hope.

Through all the bright hours
I cling to expectation, until
darkness comes to reclaim me
as its own. Hope fades, day is gone
into its irredeemable place
and I am thrown back into the familiar
bonds of disconsolation.
Gloom crawls around
lapping lasciviously
between my toes, at my ankles,
and it sucks the strands of my
hair. It forgives my heady
fling with Hope. I am
joined again into its
greedy arms.[3]

This type of hope is not an empowering energy, largely
because it seems to rely on external forces coming into play – the
help of other people, and obstacles to improvement somehow
miraculously disappearing without you having to do anything.
I want to suggest hope is a combination of attitude of mind and
action. It is the refusal to accept that how things are is how they
will always be; that even if I'm going through hell, there is more
to life than what I can see and understand. Despair needn't have
the last word. It's common sense really, because to live is to
change. The question is, will that change be for the better or

worse? Hope is the belief that it can be for the better, and even if we get knocked back or broken down, there is always a way to go forward. In other words, hope is resilience in action. It's about refusing to accept the burden and pain I, others or society may want to place upon me. It's tough, spirited and bloody-minded. Maya Angelou again conveys perfectly this type of hope in 'Still I Rise':

> You may write me down in history
> With your bitter, twisted lies,
> You may trod me in the very dirt
> But still, like dust, I'll rise.
>
> Does my sassiness upset you?
> Why are you beset with gloom?
> 'Cause I walk like I've got oil wells
> Pumping in my living room.
>
> Just like moons and like suns,
> With the certainty of tides,
> Just like hopes springing high,
> Still I'll rise.
>
> Did you want to see me broken?
> Bowed head and lowered eyes?
> Shoulders falling down like teardrops,
> Weakened by my soulful cries?
>
> Does my haughtiness offend you?
> Don't you take it awful hard
> 'Cause I laugh like I've got gold mines
> Diggin' in my own backyard.

You may shoot me with your words,
You may cut me with your eyes,
You may kill me with your hatefulness,
But still, like air, I'll rise.

Does my sexiness upset you?
Does it come as a surprise
That I dance like I've got diamonds
At the meeting of my thighs?

Out of the huts of history's shame
I rise
Up from a past that's rooted in pain
I rise
I'm a black ocean, leaping and wide,
Welling and swelling I bear in the tide.

Leaving behind nights of terror and fear
I rise
Into a daybreak that's wondrously clear
I rise
Bringing the gifts that my ancestors gave,
I am the dream and the hope of the slave.
I rise
I rise
I rise.[4]

When I embody hope I refuse to be cowed, to be defeated or broken by the crap that sometimes happens to me. I am neither drowned in self-pity nor the reproach of myself, other people, or events that have failed me. When events knock me down, I choose to regroup mentally, stand up and take the next step.

This has taken time for me to learn. I grew up in a loving family and had a wonderful and protected childhood. My expectation of life was that it would continue to be good. I was not geared to dealing with difficulty, and I have struggled much in the past when life has gone wrong. Except it hasn't gone wrong. It is simply life with all the light and shade that comes with that. Life is precarious. It is not 'fair', if by 'fair' we mean good people never suffering and bad people getting what they deserve. To live a good or wonderful life is not to have a trouble-free existence, but to transform the challenges that come our way in the normal course of events into something more life-enhancing. I've come to think that how we succeed at this depends a great deal upon our expectations.

At every step along the way as I have gone through cancer treatment, my doctors and Mairéad have let me know how a particular chemotherapy will affect me, how awful I may feel, what will happen to me, and what I can do to get through those difficult times. It has made the process 'do-able'. I've been as prepared as I can be. Debilitating fear and a sense of inadequacy have been prevented. I have weathered the storm and, having come out the other side, feel mentally stronger, even as I am still putting back together my exhausted, battered physical self. All this makes me wonder how much better it might be for our children if we helped them understand that hard knocks and tough times are part of 'normal' life, and equipped them to work through these times so that they come out as stronger and more compassionate human beings at the end.

Lived-out hope brings strength, but it may be a fragile thing. In the face of constant bad news and repeated blows it's hard to keep living hopefully. That's why, when I'm going through a personally difficult time, I ration the amount of bad news I listen to and I work to have good experiences and encounters to counter the negative, debilitating aspects of human life. I want to affirm what is life-giving, not add to what is death-dealing. Adam Zagajewski expresses this in his poem, 'Try to Praise the Mutilated World':

Try to praise the mutilated world.
Remember June's long days,
and wild strawberries, drops of rosé wine.
The nettles that methodically overgrow
the abandoned homesteads of exiles.
You must praise the mutilated world.
You watched the stylish yachts and ships;
one of them had a long trip ahead of it,
while salty oblivion awaited others.
You've seen the refugees going nowhere,
you've heard the executioners sing joyfully.
You should praise the mutilated world.
Remember the moments when we were together
in a white room and the curtain fluttered.
Return in thought to the concert where music flared.
You gathered acorns in the park in autumn
and leaves eddied over the earth's scars.
Praise the mutilated world
and the gray feather a thrush lost,
and the gentle light that strays and vanishes
and returns.[5]

Chronic crippling experience is diminishing and soul-destroying. It leaves us desiccated and, if we allow it, we reflect these destructive characteristics to the world. This in turn makes it hard for people of goodwill to come close enough to support and help us, and we end up in a downward spiral. Sometimes what we need is a mental kick up the backside to get us back on track. Even as someone who knows what it is to be a victim, and who has valued greatly the help and support of others, I can't help wondering sometimes if we are a culture that encourages states of victimhood rather than enabling people to develop resilience. There are exceptions, of course. The Invictus Games, for injured military service personnel around the world, which took place in Canada during my treatment, is a wonderful example of people who have come through great pain, despair and disability and refuse to be beaten. With the support of others they have learnt to sit or stand tall again and, mentally they're able, like the wild swans at Coole, to take flight once more.

That said, in other areas of difficult human experience sometimes the care offered doesn't empower those suffering but keeps them in a state of dependency. To listen empathetically means taking seriously the story of someone's experience and the significance it holds for them. Sometimes, it may also mean raising difficult questions for someone who has become stuck in victim status, in order to help them see other possible ways in which they might go forward.

I don't say any of this lightly. I know what it is to battle on with the everyday, appearing apparently fine while feeling brokenhearted or despairing. It's taking me a lifetime to learn to let go of destructive memories, losses, mind-sets and behaviours. I understand my sister when she speaks of her work in a food bank, and says her experience suggests that some of her customers have had such abusive or unloving starts in life at the hands of inadequate key 'carers', that she cannot see how they will ever be able to 'take up their bed and walk'. And how can people break out of cycles of poverty and deprivation if society itself is structured in a way that makes it all the harder for them to do anything other than live hand to mouth?

Yet there are plenty of examples of men and women who emerge from the most appalling circumstances and live lives that fulfil their potential and inspire others. I have come to believe that wallowing in our own woes and woundedness is not the way to live this one precious life that we have, and although I need the assistance of fellow travellers (usually of those who know the experience from the inside) to help me get out of the holes I sometimes get into, it is ultimately down to me to commit to a particular path of change. For the healed man hiding away in the temple, Jesus' words come as a sharp incentive to get him back out on the road to recovery, but ultimately recovery won't come unless the man's answer to the question, 'Do you want to be healed?' is 'Yes!'

I may not be able to help what happens to me, but I do not have to remain a victim, however much easier that may sometimes be. Nor do I want to be labelled as a 'survivor'. I want to be known as Ruth, who with the help of others may stand tall and enable them to do the same; who is not defined by the destructive things that happen to me, but by the creative choices I make and flesh out in action. We're in this together, and we all have gifts to bring. If we don't bring them, then change won't happen to the extent needed. The key is not to be dependent or independent but interdependent.

This last point needs emphasising: in the light of my experience in the Isolation Unit I would be deeply dishonest if I did not acknowledge that sometimes the anguish we experience is beyond our own capacity to heal. That's why community is so crucial, and we lose human connectedness at our peril. While the motivation for change must come from our own heart, we may often need the support and expertise of others to help us live as fully as we can.

One last point about hope: in the place of life-threatening illness I have wondered if it is possible to remain hopeful in the face of unavoidable and imminent death, should that be part of my own experience of cancer. If hope was about reaching the light at the end of the tunnel, and death is when the light goes out, how can hope flourish as the light dies? For me now, hope is not primarily about an endpoint, a happy ending, but how I travel along the way, in this moment and this moment and this moment and so on. Right up until I lose consciousness I can be thankful for the loved ones around me, the care of carers, the beauty I may still be able to glimpse around me or call to mind, the things I can do while 'doing' is still possible, and the grace I can live out as I let go of what can no longer be, and say my goodbyes. These things I can do, whether or not I believe in some kind of existence after death. Hope is about my attitudes and action in the here and now, not about a life hereafter.

10

'See, you are well!' . . . possibly

About six weeks after I left the Isolation Unit I had a CT scan. The results were not back by the time I went to clinic the following week. I was examined by a doctor I hadn't met before. Mairéad was not present. I was completely thrown and wanted to cry. I realised how much the continuity of being seen by the same doctors and Mairéad had enabled me to feel safe and stay calm. Yet their absence was a good sign. It was the first indication that I was on the mend. Rationally, I knew there were now other patients who needed my consultants' and Mairéad's attention in a way that I didn't any longer. Emotionally, I felt bereft. Although it did not occur to me at the time, later reflection made me aware that this situation indicated I was once again in a place of transition from one identity to another, from being a seriously ill patient to being a well person. I was not well yet, but I was recovering, and recovery required a shift in self-perception.

This shift was necessary because my world was opening up again and I needed to rediscover my place in it. Life as a seriously ill patient was a narrow and clearly defined existence. So much was taken out of my control. So much of my well-being depended upon the expertise and care of others. The only choice I had was how I was going to respond to living in the shadow of death. I chose to live through treatment as gratefully, calmly and graciously as was possible for me. Looking back, I felt that I had been the person I hoped I might be in such circumstances, but normal life is more messy and complicated in its demands than I found to be the case with life-threatening illness. I wondered about my ability to engage well with it, taking with me all the lessons of the last year.

The challenge to accept uncertainty was heightened by my scan results. Because these were not back when I attended clinic, the abdominal images were reviewed by all the consultants in their cross-disciplinary meeting the following day. Mairéad rang later in the afternoon to tell me the conclusion drawn from these pictures was that I was in remission. There was much rejoicing in the family but I felt unexpectedly devoid of any emotion. I'd been steeling myself for the scan result, just in case it was bad news. Perhaps I didn't quite believe it. I was still coughing and although I was so much better than a few weeks earlier, I continued to have grim days when doing anything was a struggle. I wasn't sure if this was normal, or an indication that there was a problem. I was reluctant to relax my guard, just in case . . .

The following day Mairéad called again. When the consultant radiologist went to write up the report of my scan he looked at all the images from my throat to my pelvis and observed a 17mm nodule in my liver and several smaller nodes in my lungs. These might simply be infection, he said, but he advised my doctors to keep an eye on them.

'Could they be cancer?' I asked.

'Yes.'

Back to a state of uncertainty although, in reality, I'd never lost that perspective. I knew that the cancer might persist, return or spread, and that the treatment I'd had could make me vulnerable to other cancers.

News of the abnormalities in my liver and lungs unsettled me for a couple of days, but when I regained my emotional balance I was conscious of a shift that had happened since I first became ill just over a year ago. In the beginning, uncertainty was what I had found the hardest to cope with. It caused me anxiety and left me feeling vulnerable. Now it was part of my emotional landscape. I knew that as a result of this cancer the only certainties I had in my life are that one day I will die, and that I am loved. These were, and are, enough.

Antoine de Saint-Exupéry wrote, 'Perfection is achieved not when there is nothing more to add, but when there is nothing left to take away.'[1] I am far from being perfect, but my gap year caused me to let go of so many expectations and perceptions that ceased to be accurate or important in the light of life-threatening illness. There was liberation in this letting go.

Finding freedom in loosening my grip on any certainty that I'd live even to the end of the year, let alone any longer, was harder to realise than the liberty that comes from relinquishing many other 'certainties'. Yet, somehow, I'd made it through to a psychological space in which I could sit comfortably with my mortality, imminent or otherwise. I could rejoice in the day, and there was not one that went by without me feeling thankful for the gift of it. Uncertainty about whether a long or short life lay ahead of me meant that, from that point, gratitude for each day would be part of the bedrock of my existence. Death and love aside, I took nothing for granted.

If feeling 'at home' with life was linked with being emotionally impregnable and certain about its meaning and purpose, then I'd be forever homeless, and that was okay. I knew the importance of being vulnerable, of travelling light. Feeling at home was no longer about external contexts, but internal ease. This sense of ease was characterised by an acceptance of uncertainty, insecurity and fragility, recognising that these are not negatives to be feared but realities to be lived out courageously and gracefully. Of course, it was both that simple and not that simple!

If thankfulness for life had become the conscious backdrop of my outlook, the question remained about how I lived each day, uncertain as I was about whether or not I'd be alive for long. How much work should I book in? If my time was limited, should I accept invitations that I might have to withdraw from if my health nose-dived? What should the balance of work and leisure be? How should I re-engage when some days I felt fine and others I struggled physically to get through the day? Should I live as if I were fully in remission until either symptoms or the next scan result indicated that was not the case?

At that time, I chose to answer yes to the last question. The amount of work I booked was academic since I did not have the energy to take on huge amounts, and although invitations were beginning to come in again, I was not being inundated with them. What work I did have was manageable. I trusted that as I recovered and was capable of doing more, more would emerge.

One of the unforeseen challenges of recovery was holding the tension between the deep gratitude I felt daily for still being alive while also feeling frustrated and sad about my physical limitations, particularly on the days when I was less well. It seemed churlish to resent slow progress when, without treatment, I would not be alive, but I struggled to accept this in-between stage in which my concentration was compromised and my energy levels depleted to varying degrees. I felt more self-pity about my situation, and shed more tears over it, than was the case all the way through the illness, diagnosis and treatment. I felt more useless at this point, when I was able to do some bits of work, than I did when I was incapable of doing anything. I didn't know when the right response to weariness was to rest, and when it was to do that little bit more so I could build up my strength gradually again.

As a freelancer I could accommodate the 'up and down' nature of my days, working when I was able to, and resting when that was necessary, but if I was working with a group over a few days I couldn't opt out when exhaustion kicked in and my concentration flagged. Without work I had no income, and my reserves had rapidly diminished over the previous twelve months. I could feel the pressure to earn building up. How was it possible to hold the heightened sense of the preciousness of life, while acknowledging the struggles and basic demands of some days? I wanted to be neither ungrateful nor an inauthentic Pollyanna, forever presenting a positive front while feeling deeply downcast within.

Alongside these challenges I was conscious of the desire to make changes in my life that began to address some of the issues about 'normal' life I'd become aware of in the shadow of death. I'd noted personal and societal perceptions and behaviours that may be the norm, but which are inhumane. These continue to diminish or destroy our capacity to live life fully, to enable others to do the same, and to care for our environment. I recognised that I needed to change some of my attitudes and actions, and challenge some of the dehumanising perceptions, practices and politics in wider society. What I was not sure about was quite how to do that.

Today we are faced by crises of such magnitude that I might conclude the only way forward is to mobilise movements for change, or join existing movements that I think are working effectively to transform our abuse of the Earth. I want to make my voice heard among millions of others calling for radical and essential rethinking and reacting in relation to environmental issues and international politics and policies that increase the threat of violent conflict within and between nations. I want to work in ways that make me part of the solution, not the problem. But I am also wary of becoming involved in movements.

Back in the August of my gap year, during a brief spell at home between chemotherapy sessions, my eye was caught by a question posed by Quaker Maud Grainger, on the cover of *the Friends Quarterly* magazine: 'Do we want to build a movement for a transformed world that works for all, and is such a movement possible?'[2] Grainger wrote about a course she had attended, 'that spoke to relentless persistence . . . I believe we can be part of a movement that talks and listens to all people, where we may not all agree but can find ways to engage with others.'[3] I have found this to be true, but life becomes much more complicated as the membership of a movement grows, and the formalisation of informal groups working for positive change requires various bureaucratic hoops to be navigated.

I know from experience that funders are often goal-driven. That's understandable. They want tangible results to come from their investment in a project, but anyone working with the legacy of violent conflict, for example, knows that positive outcomes may not be immediate, and that a considerable amount of work and time is often required in building or enabling the essential relationships that pave the way to positive transformation.

As movements grow there are more regulations to fulfil in terms of charitable status, safeguarding or employment law. These are important but they're also time-consuming and they divert energy and resources away from fulfilling the vision that created the movement for change in the first place. What energy I do have I want to use responding to the problems that concern me, not the internal conflicts and politics of charitable groups. I recognise these unhelpful dynamics are inevitable, given that none of us is perfect, but I'm cautious about getting involved with them.

While I was working on this book, a number of national and international charities hit the headlines because a few of their staff had abused their position of power and taken sexual advantage of vulnerable people they were supposed to be supporting. Because of their abusive actions many thousands of people withdrew their financial support. Those who suffered as a result were not primarily the staff who behaved inappropriately, but the people who needed aid, and the non-abusive charity workers who might be met with hostility and fear as a result of their colleagues' abusive actions. Energy that could have been used to support those struggling to survive was needed in the aftermath of the revelations to respond to the public outcry that resulted and to develop policies and practices that prevented further sexual exploitation as far as possible.

We need organisations and movements but, I realised, that was no longer where I wanted to direct my energy. I was drawn simply to doing what needed to be done in those spheres where I could effect change in my own backyard, or within my wider field of work. Early on in my illness I was moved by an article about Jean Vanier, the founder of L'Arche. Vanier was invited to visit an asylum for men with learning disabilities. He was appalled by what he saw. He visited other asylums before deciding to invite two of the men to live with him.

'There was no huge idea,' he says, 'no intention to change the world.' He simply wanted to ease the suffering of two men.[4] Vanier did what he was able to do. He found his life was as enriched by the men as their lives were by living with him. His act caught the imagination of others, and new communities developed where adults with learning difficulties lived with people drawn from the whole wider community to the benefit and learning of all. There are a hundred and forty-seven L'Arche communities today, spread across thirty-five countries.

I was drawn to Vanier's example because he didn't set out to do anything more than make a positive difference within his own means. He had the humility to know he couldn't change the world but, somehow, through his life, the world of those belonging to L'Arche communities has been changed, and the ripples spread out so that others, like me, are inspired to respond as we are able to the needs we recognise around us.

Not that I was able to do very much at the time these reflections came to me. I was only just beginning to do creative work again, and I found I was easily knocked by demands which, prior to my illness, I wouldn't have thought about twice. I had days of feeling more distressed and dispirited than I did at any point during treatment. The only way I could make sense of why that was so was expressed in an email to my friend, Richard:

> I have never thought of myself as 'battling' cancer – I think that imagery is unhelpful because when someone dies of cancer, they're seen as 'losing the battle' while the way they lived their last days and died may have been a great triumph and tribute to the human spirit – but the present experience feels like that of soldiers returning from the arena of violent conflict who, having functioned well through their deployment, suddenly find the traumatic legacy of those experiences catching up with them just at the same time as they are having to readjust to 'home' reality with its wider demands. Life both is and isn't the same as it was before they went away. They both are and aren't the same person they were before they were called up to face a different and challenging reality.

Life wasn't the same because, confronted by my own mortality and the possible imminence of dying, everyday life had taken on a different meaning. I experienced it as a gift, not a drudge, something to be constantly savoured and given thanks for. But life was also the same, with some days being mundane, ordinary days, and nothing to get excited about. Visiting an old book barn, I noticed a blue tile at the entrance proclaiming, 'ON THIS SITE, SEPT 5 1782, NOTHING HAPPENED'. I have those days. Perhaps I could sit more easily with them than I did before I was ill, or perhaps not. Despite my best intentions I found familiar neurotic responses I thought I'd laid to rest now re-emerging as I picked up the reins of normal life again.

Perhaps, though, I could respond to them with a little more grace, understanding, acceptance and humour. This is me! This complex, beautiful being who has weathered treatment well, yet carries no illusions about her frailties and failings; who, in trying to preserve her dignity, for example, ended up losing it completely, crouched Gollum-like on top of the hospital toilet, trying to sort out by herself the impacted bowel that ultimately only a nurse-given enema could ease! The image makes me laugh every time I recall that grim moment when my only option was to pull the 'Nurse Call' cord in the toilet and, when she came, to waddle back to bed wearing an incontinence sheet like a nappy, so she could force an enema up 'where the sun don't shine'. You don't see too many of those images in stained-glass windows! Sadly, but not unexpectedly, I had not become a saint through living with cancer and its treatment, but I think I have become more deeply human and humane. I can forgive my flaws a little more easily: life is too short to waste it wishing I were a better person than I am, rather than rejoicing that I 'am' at all.

As for uncertainty, thank God for it! Without it there would be no questions to explore, no deeper realities to plumb, no adventure to be had, no risks to be taken, no thrill of living. Cancer isn't all bad. It has thrown my life into sharp relief, focusing my attention on what matters, and giving me the chance to make sure those I love know how much I love them. It has enabled me to relinquish some negative perceptions and to sit more easily with who I am. Even as I became frustrated with the post-treatment legacy of physical and psychological limitations, a voice inside was also telling me how bloody marvellous I had been, and still am. It may only be a faint voice, but it wasn't there before, and I'm tickled pink by its presence.

I know now I am not afraid of dying. If cancer ends my life, when it's my turn I shall slip away to the sound of music. A recent radio programme reminded me of Seamus Heaney's poem, 'At the Wellhead'. It refers to an ageing and beloved singer in his life who has now departed, and whom he urges to 'Sing yourself to where the singing comes from'.[5] I love that image! That's how I want to let go of life, singing, or listening to others singing. I will grieve the beloved ones I leave behind – they are so dear to me – but cancer will have given me, has already given me, time to tell them all I need to say. I will not be snatched away with no word of farewell.

If I am able to live for a number of years yet, then that's what I'll continue to do passionately – LIVE. I was drawn by the title of Dawna Markova's book, *I Will Not Die an Unlived Life*.[6] I know what it is to have lived, to have experienced joy and completeness, to be caught up in beauty, and to have felt free. I reaffirm my desire not to live an indifferent life, ignoring or ignorant about the death-dealing situations others are forced to endure. I will not be afraid to try and fail and try again; to step out in faith, uncertain where my path is leading; prepared to live the questions rather than settle for easy answers I know to be inadequate. I want to be a source of inspiration rather than exasperation to those whose lives touch mine and to continue learning from them until the day I die. I owe it not only to myself and the family and friends who have loved me through this time, but also to those women with life-threatening cancers, some of them now dead, with whom I've shared this experience. I owe it also to the amazing lymphoma team and nurses at Southampton General Hospital who have given me life I would not have had without their expertise. On my dismal days I picture Mairéad saying, 'See, you are well!' and encouraging me gently but firmly to get back out into life.

Today I sit easily with the thought that this life may well be all there is. Any other reality beyond it is also beyond my comprehension and expectation. My faith teaches me to focus on the here and now, not the hereafter, on this moment when I can be the best 'me' possible; when I live fully in the present, neither regretting the past that's gone, nor fearing a future that may never happen.

I'm aware of so many destructive human energies in the world; energies that seek not to build up our common life, but to lay waste to it. I imagine and experience a greater creative energy suffusing our lives, countering our capacity for needless destruction and hatred, and inspiring those who choose to live loving, compassionate lives. I might call this energy 'God', although I do so with some reluctance because the word has so many unhelpful accretions attached to it now. Too many of those who use it do so to exclude others who are living out profound love but do not feel the need to call their inspiration 'God'.

My ability to sit with and rejoice in mystery has grown through this last year. I cannot say whether the source of the calmness and gratitude I've felt as I travelled through the valley of the shadow of death is the result of anything more than the human care I've received and my own attitude of mind. I only know I've felt it. I notice but do not need to explain those moments of suddenly being aware I'm standing on holy ground in encounters with other patients or with the nurses and doctors caring for me. I love the fact that without promptings from me, the books, papers, essays or words of encouragement friends sent or recommended to me, have tied in with what I happened to be writing at the time. Coincidence, or synchronicity? It doesn't matter what you call it. It's what I have experienced.

It seems to me that what matters most is not what happens to us, but how we perceive what happens to us, and how we choose to respond to those perceptions. I have chosen not to see my cancer as an enemy to be fought, but as an impersonal biological development in my body that requires treatment and may teach me much along the way. I think of the cancer as neither good nor bad. It just is, and because of it I have been on a pilgrimage exploring yet another aspect of what it means to be human. Without doubt this particular pilgrimage has sometimes brought me to my knees, challenged my sense of self and the world, confronted me with painful questions and the possibility of unwelcome outcomes. I have not always been calm and collected or grateful for this unexpected education. I have sometimes cried and struggled unedifyingly, in bad humour and with limited resilience.

The notion of pilgrimage implies a holy place as the destination of what may be a long and demanding walk. I am unclear about the length of my pilgrimage with cancer, or its endpoint. During the latter months of treatment a biblical story came to mind that held resonance for me. The book of Genesis introduces us to the patriarch Jacob. One of the things I love about the Hebrew scriptures is that their heroes are not stained-glass saints but very flesh-and-blood, flawed human beings. Jacob, aided and abetted by his mother, is a deceptive character who dupes his father and twin brother and is sent away from home in fear of his life. So begins a pilgrimage that will ultimately bring him full circle to facing the threats that caused his earlier flight from home.

Early on in the journey Jacob finds himself in a rather barren place where he spends the night. Despite having only a rock as a pillow, he manages to fall asleep. As he sleeps, he dreams of a ladder connecting heaven and earth, of angels ascending and descending the ladder and his God assuring him that whatever happens, ultimately all will be well. When he wakes up Jacob says, 'Surely the Lord is in this place – and I did not know it!'[7]

For Jacob, a desolate place becomes the space in which he unexpectedly encounters God. I am less clear about, and uncomfortable with, the word and its meaning, but I have encountered holiness in the sometimes desolate landscape of cancer and its treatment. By 'holiness' I mean moments when I am lost for words and all I can feel is a sense of awe and wonder. It's not what I expected but it's what I experienced. For that, I am truly grateful. As in Jacob's story, this sudden awareness of the sacredness that is the essence of life, not separate from it, is not a neat ending, but a point of encouragement along a difficult route of repeated mistakes and moments of insight, of contradictions, paradoxes and complexity.

As I gradually attend to the changes in behaviour and action that now seem necessary to me, I also want to continue paying attention to the more-than-me-ness of life, or, as Malcolm Guite puts it in his blog, 'that mysterious moment of awareness, assent and transformation in which eternity touches time'.[8] These moments are all too easily missed, but they make such a difference. It seems to me that at the point of something new gestating in my life, even if it turns out simply to be the opening words of that life's final chapter, what feeds my soul is poetry and art, music and myth-making. There are no wise words to finish, because I'm not yet finished. To whatever comes I say, YES, and hope I will rise to the challenge with as much grace and humour as I can muster. So be it.

Epilogue

In July of the year following my gap year, about eight months after I completed all the treatment available to me, I was readmitted to hospital with a very painful dose of shingles. The rash covered my sacral and genital areas. The only comfortable position was lying on my front. I spent a week in isolation receiving antiviral drugs intravenously. The windows in my room were too high and too dirty to see through. The only picture in the white-walled room was a photo of autumn, with damp and blotched yellow leaves and little beauty. It spoke of death, not life. I felt like a caged animal.

A week after I was admitted I was due to go home, but my expected morning release time was unnecessarily delayed for many hours. The doctor had forgotten to sign my discharge papers, which meant they couldn't be sent to pharmacy for my drugs. My distress and despair were palpable. In that week I seemed to have lost the calm and gratitude that characterised most of my previous times in hospital. I hung on to the Prof's words from a few days earlier, when he spoke of shingles doing strange things to one's mind as well as body. That rang so true. I felt wretched.

As the minutes passed by it seemed like my mental anguish began to affect me physically. During this time of extended waiting, when I should already have made it home, the Prof came to see me on his ward round. I emerged from the toilet as he walked through the door, and staggered into him. I was half carried to the bed, as the world spun. Within an hour I was vomiting copious amounts of black/green fluid. The next day I started passing blood. I remained in hospital for another three weeks. There was concern that the lymphoma might have returned. I was introduced to the gentle palliative care team doctor for advice around pain relief and, I suspect, to begin to build the kind of relationship that might be needed in the event of end-of-life care. The possibility of becoming part of an immunotherapy clinical trial was discussed, and preparations relating to this began in earnest. This would be my last chance. Investigations and abdominal surgery to examine and extract biopsies of various tissues necessitated a move upstairs into isolation on the Critical Care ward. The reality that I might only have a few months to live loomed large.

One thought struck me forcibly, even as I lived through that traumatic month. It was to recognise how my assessment of the delay in my discharge from hospital changed dramatically as that day unfolded. Initially I judged it to be a complete disaster but, after I was taken ill, I was immensely relieved that I was still on the ward. How awful to get home only to plaster the living room in vile vomit, and be rushed back into hospital! The delay remained a delay, but my attitude was transformed by the bigger picture. Although I am struggling to articulate it, I feel there is something of importance here. It is to do with understanding my limitations of perception and the unhelpful judgements that often accompany that narrowness of vision: the kneejerk reactions I have to immediate experiences, determining them to be good or bad, positive or negative, creative or destructive, without taking the time to consider them as part of a bigger picture.

The result of plumping for a particular limited interpretation is that I invest it with meaning and emotion which may be detrimental, blocking me from navigating my way through it, particularly if circumstances change and my original take on what's happened is challenged, as in the story I've recalled of my delayed discharge. Part of the reason this particular month in hospital was such an emotional rollercoaster was that I tried to embrace each new piece of the jigsaw without really knowing how the different elements might ultimately come together. When the complication of shingles was followed by symptoms suggesting the lymphoma had returned and I might only live a few months, I squared up to that prognosis and decided it was probably a *good* outcome: I'm too much of a cissy to cope well with the growing limitations and frustrations of old age. When that diagnosis became more doubtful I found it frightening to think that I might, after all, outlive Chris. I was unprepared for such an outcome and, as a result, at first it felt almost like bad news.

In the early days after I was discharged finally from that month in hospital, I began editing this book. I noted how, at the time I wrote the first chapter, I had accepted the cancer simply as, 'life evolving in all its creative and destructive complexity'. Eighteen months further down the line, more recent experience has made me wonder at my judgement of the cancer being 'destructive'. It had changed the course of my life, for sure, but I could no longer say it was a *bad* thing. I had learnt so much, faced so much, felt so much, and found healing for deeply important but damaged relationships in my life, all as a result of this life-threatening lymphoma. What this suggests is that the way forward was not to get caught up with immediate adjustments and value judgements in relation to what happened to me on a daily basis, but to make room for the

'God's-eye view'. The archetypal story in the book of Job came to mind, with my experience enabling me to understand it in a different way.

Through the myth of Job ancient writers wrestled with the presence of suffering in the world, and the question of why innocent and good people suffer. This aspect of the story is not the one that interests me here. I consider myself to be neither innocent nor good! What captured my imagination was how Job and his three 'friends' respond to all the catastrophes, humiliations, diseases, bereavements and material losses that beset him. Each reacts to the immediate situation, making value judgements about unfolding events. The three friends see Job as responsible for what has happened to him. They think he can't have been as righteous as he appeared to be. Somehow he must have offended their God and now he's paying the price. Job is also caught up with trying to make sense of what's happening to him. Initially, he stands up for his integrity of being, prays for relief, rails against the violence of life, is overcome with self-pity and despair, and struggles to keep faith with his God. It's exhausting. In reality, though each character thinks he is an expert on life and the meaning of it, all four, like me, know barely anything in the general scheme of things.

The crunch point comes in the story when their God enters the conversation. 'Who is this that darkens counsel by words without knowledge? . . . Where were you when I laid the foundation of the earth? . . .'[1] In other words, all the accusations and agonising are futile. It's utterly understandable that we want to make sense of the experiences we have, but our limitations of vision can lead us to misleading conclusions.

During my treatment, I was reminded on a couple of occasions of Job's friends. For me they came in the form of well-meaning non-medical professionals. The first, who, on hearing my diagnosis, informed me that cancer was her area of expertise, went on to say that those who developed the disease cared for others but not themselves. This, too, was the perspective of the second stranger, who patted my hand, smiled pityingly and said, 'Who hasn't been looking after herself!'

I took both women to task. We know there are lifestyle factors in a number of cancers, but that's only part of the picture. Take lung cancer as an example. There are people who smoke like chimneys who don't get the disease and others who develop it who don't smoke at all. There are many contributory elements to why some of us become ill and others remain healthy – our genes, places of birth and growth, social circumstances, environmental context, to name but a few. We have no control over some of these. It's far too simplistic, not to say insensitive, to blame people for the illnesses that suddenly overtake them.

'Do you think telling me, however nicely, that I am responsible for the lymphoma I have, is helpful to me?' I asked.

I realised that investing emotional energy in short-sighted interpretations that later prove inadequate is a waste of my reserves. Lying in my hospital bed my imagination was caught by a phrase my friend Chris uses during his Radio 2 Breakfast Show. He talked about the value of 'dancing the changes'. The image appealed to me very much. I think that's what I managed to do relatively well during my gap year. Yet the more I reflected on it, the less honest I felt I was being with myself. I knew that I had found that most recent month in hospital and its aftermath the hardest to cope with. I missed Mairéad. I missed the familiar safety and wonderful staff on ward D3. I felt oppressed by my single room with its high and filthy windows. I felt unwell and out of control, and I struggled emotionally to keep my head above water. A dream I had, after we finally learnt in the outpatient clinic that all three biopsies were clear of lymphoma, captured the sense of dislocation triggered by that time.

It was a dream within a dream. I was swimming between islands off the north coast of Scotland. I had almost made it to shore when a rip current caught hold of me and whirled me out to sea so rapidly that all I could do was shout for help as I skimmed past other swimmers, out of my depth and further and further away from solid ground. I 'awoke' from this dream to find I was lying in bed between my mum and one of my sisters, both leaning over me, concerned about my cries for help. My mum has been dead for a few years, so the image was of me held between life and death, and not knowing which way to turn. At this point I woke up properly.

In hospital, as I struggled to keep myself psychologically afloat, and tried not to get sucked into the depths of depression, my friend Nicky came unwittingly to my rescue. I knew I was in her thoughts, and that she had wondered over the months what to say to me, but we had not been in touch for a while. Then, as I was floundering around mentally, a card arrived from her. It depicted a black and white photo of a lighthouse with the spray of monumental waves crashing all around and above it. The elemental power of the waves was soul-stirring to see. The lighthouse, standing to the fore, paradoxically looked both solid and shadow-like. Inside the card Nicky had written the following poem:

A lighthouse is not built on easy ground,
on sunlit uplands, safe and fertile land,
but in wild places where most danger's found
craggy outcrops, rock-spits, soft sinking-sand;
where hard earth, wild winds, icy waters meet.
In some grand and elemental showdown.
Survival is a monumental feat.
You know that someone else would sink or drown.
But still we want you to transcend it all,

to bathe us in your steady brilliance.
A lighthouse never falters, cannot fall,
exhausts itself in tough self-reliance.
Your weakest light is brightest in the darkest night.
May what inspires us, help you keep us in your sight.[2]

I was profoundly moved by Nicky's words. Incredibly, she was likening me to the vulnerable power of the lighthouse withstanding the fiercest storm. She seemed to see me as an inspiration, and she wanted me to be aware of those around me willing me to keep burning with life. I had all but lost touch with the strength that she associated with me. Her card and poem called me back to that aspect of who I am. I kept it by my bed and reread it many times. Today it is on my desk, encouraging me to hold steady.

Since Nicky first sent her card I have been back in hospital twice more. The first time, a perforation in my intestine leading to peritonitis resulted in an emergency ambulance admission to my local hospital, further surgery, a stay in Intensive Care, and the prospect of further abdominal complications and surgical interventions. I knew the humiliation of waking up in a pool of bloody faeces, and drenched in drainage fluid from tubes in my abdomen. I knew the fear of eating because I wasn't sure what pain or emergency problems might be provoked by one food type or another.

A couple of weeks after I was discharged I managed to make it up to BBC Radio 2 to do my 'Pause for Thought' slot on the Chris Evans Breakfast Show. The night before the broadcast we were staying with a friend in Richmond. When I went to bed I realised that what I thought was a pulled muscle in my right leg was probably a deep vein thrombosis. My calf had swollen. I agonised about what to do. Should I return to hospital immediately or go ahead with my 'Pause for Thought' the next day? With some anxiety I opted for the latter. My friend, Paul, drove me door to door in the morning so I didn't have to navigate tube trains and a lot of walking. As soon as we returned to Richmond, Chris and I set off back to Southampton. I went straight to the lymphoma clinic. An ultrasound confirmed I had multiple clots in my right leg. I was admitted to the Oncology ward.

As the afternoon progressed, the abdominal pain that had not ceased since my previous surgery increased. By the evening it had become unbearable. Then I started vomiting copious amounts of fresh blood. The next few hours were a blur. I was convinced I was going to die. I was aware of doctors and Critical Care staff trying to access my veins. I went into shock. For the first time in all the treatment, I felt I lost it completely. I felt frightened and panicked. I remember Chris's calm voice, and those of the Critical Care Outreach nurses, but I couldn't steady myself. I tried not to cry out but I was unable to be helpful in any way. I later learned I had lost a great deal of blood during that time. I remember coming to with the pain under some degree of control. At some point I went to theatre and had a section of intestine removed. I returned to consciousness in the Intensive Care Unit with tubes emerging from every orifice and a Frankenstein incision on my abdomen with fine tubing inserted around the surgery.

The surgeons and ICU staff had saved my life, but what struck me about the experience was that it was utterly different from all the treatment of the previous year. It confirmed everything I had written about control, fear, uncertainty and dying, except that the death I expected on that awful night was the antithesis of the one I felt I might welcome if my cancer got the better of me. It would not have been a gentle letting go, but a fear- and pain-filled last few hours. Freya and Tian would learn about it with shock, and Chris would remember it as a time of anguish when he held calm while I covered him in blood and was unable to be coherent in any way, except to beg him to contact the Prof. All this has reminded me of the importance of having a good death.

My sister, Ann, suggested that although I was not with it for some of that time, the will to live must have persisted. Who knows? Like the month in the Isolation Unit, I could only struggle through it, held by the human love and skill around me. If I had been in a reflective mood I might have felt the sentiment, 'My God, my God, why have you forsaken me?', but I was utterly in the present moment of simply struggling to survive.

The more I've thought about it subsequently, the more conscious I am of not being disturbed by a seeming absence of God. There are three main reasons for this. Firstly, I no longer believe in a God who is personally concerned for, but separate from me. Secondly, I share Teilhard de Chardin's understanding that matter and spirit 'are two *states* or two aspects of one and the same cosmic Stuff . . .'[3] For me this means that the energy some call God is the essence of all that is, more than, yet not separate from me. This means I do not experience it as 'another' who is present or absent. Thirdly, the Source of all Being is beyond my understanding, whether my life feels good or is crippling. My task is to be as open as possible to the mystery and energy of life, not to pin it down in inadequate images.

Perhaps at some future point ultimate reality will become clear, or loss of consciousness will render clarity unnecessary. My energy will simply be taken up into the energy of the universe, mingling with that of all who have gone before.

As I complete the final edits for this book, I am in and out of hospital. The section of intestine removed most recently showed live lymphoma. I am undergoing further chemotherapy with the possibility of a donor stem cell transplant. I may become part of an immunotherapy clinical trial. I may be cured, or I may find there is nothing more to be done, and enter end-of-life care. The uncertainty goes on, yet Nicky's image of the lighthouse remains inspirational to me.

Lighthouses stand tall and unwavering in all kinds of seas; in calm swells as well as catastrophic storms. Most comforting of all, as I have learnt on this journey through the shadow of death, 'their weakest light is brightest in the darkest night'. I do not know what length of life remains for me, but until that spark is finally snuffed out, I intend to keep burning as brightly as I am able, through whatever challenges come my way. Sometimes I may have to endure the unendurable. In such moments I must trust that others still see my weakest light, even as I fear it has been extinguished. The rest of the time I hope simply to give and receive love. In the end, that is all that really matters.

Two additional poems

I've chosen two poems below that are key for me at this time, but which didn't make it into the body of the book. For most of my life faith has been a mystery. When confronted by my own mortality I have found many people want to give me certainties, but these inevitably fall short of experience. I find great comfort in 'Via Negativa' by R.S. Thomas. His words allow for doubt, absence and uncertainty while also making room for mystery and understanding beyond rational limitations.

Why no! I never thought other than
That God is that great absence
In our lives, the empty silence
Within, the place where we go
Seeking, not in hope to
Arrive or find. He keeps the interstices
In our knowledge, the darkness
Between stars. His are the echoes
We follow, the footprints he has just
Left. We put our hands in

His side hoping to find
It warm. We look at people
And places as though he had looked
At them, too; but miss the reflection.

Wendell Berry's 'The Peace of Wild Things' is one I have carried everywhere with me for many years now. I find in the simple reciting of it that it calms my spirit and brings me peace.

When despair for the world grows in me
and I wake in the night at the least sound
in fear of what my life and my children's lives may be,
I go and lie down where the wood drake
rests in his beauty on the water, and the great heron feeds.
I come into the peace of wild things
who do not tax their lives with forethought
of grief. I come into the presence of still water.
And I feel above me the day-blind stars
waiting with their light. For a time
I rest in the grace of the world, and am free.

Afterword

Ruth was re-admitted to hospital in January 2019 with the flu. When she was well enough to have a PET scan, it revealed that her lymphoma had returned and that she had only weeks to live. She was wonderfully cared for on ward D3 and died peacefully on 20 February with her family around her. Whilst still able to, she recorded a moving interview with Chris Evans which went viral as a podcast.

As an act of gratitude to D3, Ruth's daughter Freya set up a Just Giving page to raise money for a 'Cuddle Bed' that allows those in the last stages of life to be physically close to their loved ones. Please see *www.justgiving.com/crowdfunding/freya-scott-1* for details.

Chris Scott
July 2019

Notes

Introduction

[1] Romans 8:26.

[2] Duffy, C.A., *New Selected Poems 1984–2004* (London: Picador, 2011) p. 137.

Chapter 1: Living with uncertainty

[1] Teilhard de Chardin, P., *Le Milieu Divin* (London: William Collins Sons and Co. Ltd, 1960), p. 68.

[2] Taken from an unpublished paper, 'What if . . . a paper concerning uncertainty', by Melanie Gibson 2010. Printed with her kind permission.

[3] Toynbee, P., *Part of a Journey: An Autobiographical Journal 1977–1979* (London: Collins, 1981), p. 160.

[4] Tillich, P., *The Shaking of the Foundations* (New York: Charles Scribner's Sons, 1948), Chapter 19.

[5] Thomas, R.S., *Collected Poems 1945–1990* (London: Orion Publishing, 2000), p. 199.

[6] Vanstone, W.H., *The Stature of Waiting* (London: DLT Ltd, 2004).

[7] Vanstone, *The Stature of Waiting*, p. 50.

[8]   Quoted in Friedman, L., & Moon, S. (eds), *being bodies: Buddhist women on the paradox of embodiment* (Boston: Shambhala, 1997), p. 5.

[9]   Partington, M., *If You Sit Very Still* (Bristol: Vala Publishing Cooperative, 2012), p. 24.

[10] Hawking, S., 'My life in Physics', delivered at Cambridge University at the author's seventy-fifth birthday celebrations in July 2017.

Chapter 2: Making space

[1]   cummings, e.e., *selected poems 1923–1958* (London: Faber & Faber, 1960), p. 92.

[2]   Vanstone, *The Stature of Waiting*, p. 107.

[3]   Kafka, F., *Letters to Friends, Family & Editors* (New York, Schocken Books, 1977) pp. 11–12.

[4]   Ratushinskaya, I., *Pencil Letter* (London: Hutchinson 1988), p. 27.

Chapter 3: Losing control

[1]   In Astley, N. (ed.) *Staying Alive* (Tarset: Bloodaxe Books, 2002), p. 122.

[2]   Matthew 19: 16–22.

[3]   Scott, C., *Goodbye to God* (London: Spiffing Covers, 2015), p. 27.

[4]   St John of the Cross, 'Ascent of Mount Carmel', Book 1, Chapter 13, Verse 11.

Chapter 4: Facing our fears

[1]   Mark 5: 1–13.

[2]   Kafka, *Letters to Friends, Family and Editors*, p. 10.

[3]   Dillard, A., *Pilgrim at Tinker Creek* (Norwich: Canterbury Press, 2011), p. 11.

[4]   Thomas, D., *Everyman's Poetry* (London: Everyman, 1997), p. 94.

[5]   Kafka, *Letters to Friends, Family and Editors*, p. 9.

[6]   In Astley, N. (ed.), *Being Alive* (Tarset: Bloodaxe Books, 2004), p. 258.

[7]   In Phillips, C. (ed.), *The Oxford Authors: Gerard Manley Hopkins* (Oxford: Oxford University Press, 1986), p. 170.

Chapter 5: Who am I?

[1] McCrum, R., *Every Third Thought* (London: Picador, 2017), p. 82.

[2] Ondaatje, M., *The English Patient* (London: Picador, 1992), p. 261.

[3] Rilke, R.M., tr. S. Cohn, *Sonnets to Orpheus* with *Letters to a Young Poet* (Carcanet: Manchester, 2000).

[4] Gore, A., *The Assault on Reason* (London: Bloomsbury, 2007).

[5] Gore, *The Assault on Reason*, p. 99.

[6] Gore, *The Assault on Reason*, p. 23.

[7] Gore, *The Assault on Reason*, p. 24.

[8] Sheeler, J., *Little Sparta: A Guide to the Garden of Ian Hamilton Finlay* (Edinburgh: Birlinn, 2015), p. xxv.

[9] Gore, A., *Earth in the Balance* (London: Earthscan, 2007), p. 1.

[10] Gore, *Earth in the Balance*, p. 34.

Chapter 6: Separate and shared storylines

[1] Tillich, P., *The Shaking of the Foundations*, Chapter 19.

[2] From an interview with Maggie Ferguson, reported in *The Tablet*, 19/26 August 2017, p. 6.

[3] From an interview with Tim Jonze, reported in the *Guardian* magazine, 19 August 2017 (<https://www.theguardian.com/lifeandstyle/2017/aug/19/irvine-welsh-you-see-the-white-male-rage-of-begbie-in-the-culture-today>).

[4] Jones, S., *Burn After Writing* (London: Carpet Bombing Culture, 2014), p. 15.

[5] Mantel, H., *A Place of Greater Safety* (London: Fourth Estate, 2010), p. 9.

[6] Boyle, G., *Tattoos on the Heart* (New York: Free Press, 2010), p. 54.

[7] Grashow, A., Heifetz, R. and Linsky, M., *The Practice of Adaptive Leadership* (Boston: Harvard Business Press, 2009), p. 22.

Chapter 7: To be or not to be . . .

[1] Martin Rees writing in the *i* newspaper, 1 September 2017, p. 17.

[2] 1 Corinthians 13:12.

[3] Mantel, H., *A Place of Greater Safety*, p. 49.

[4] Taken from an unpublished paper, 'Spirit and Matter', by Melanie Gibson, August 2017. Printed with her kind permission.

[5] Pylkkänen, P., *Mind, Matter and Active Information: The Relevance of David Bohm's Interpretation of Quantum Theory to Cognitive Science*. (Helsinki: Yliopistopaino, 1992).

[6] Mantel, H., *A Place of Greater Safety*, p. 205.

[7] Oliver, M., *New and Selected Poems, Volume 1* (Boston: Beacon Press, 1992), p. 94.

Chapter 8: Hitting the depths

[1] From a leader article by Tom Bawden, science correspondent, reported in the *i* newspaper, 20 November 2017, p. 20. He was commenting on original research reported in *Cancer,* and undertaken by Dr Mei Hsein Chan.

[2] Yeats, W. B., *Selected Poems* (London: Penguin Classics, 2000), p. 85.

[3] Genesis 50:20.

[4] Luke 8:45–48.

Chapter 9: Now what?

[1] John 5:2–15.

[2] Partington, M., *If You Sit Very Still*, p. 75.

[3] Angelou, M., *And Still I Rise* (London: Virago, 1986), p. 76.

[4] Angelou, *And Still I Rise*, p. 41.

[5] Zagajewski, A., tr. Clare Cavanagh, *Without End: New and Selected Poems* (New York: Farrar, Straus & Giroux, 2002), p. 60.

Chapter 10: 'See, you are well!' . . . possibly

[1] de Saint-Exupéry, A., tr. Lewis Galantière, *Wind, Sand and Stars* (London: Harcourt, 1939, 1967).

[2] Stoller, T. (ed.), *The Friends Quarterly*, No. 3, 2017 (London: The Friend Publications, 2017).

[3]   Stoller, *The Friends Quarterly*, p. 7.

[4]   Jean Vanier interviewed by Maggie Ferguson, as reported in *The Tablet*, Vol. 271, No. 9214, 19/26 August 2017, p. 6.

[5]   Heaney, S., *New Selected Poems 1988–2013* (London: Faber & Faber, 2014), p. 106.

[6]   Markova, D., *I Will Not Die an Unlived Life* (Boston: Conari Press, 2000).

[7]   Genesis 28:16.

[8]   Anite, M., 'A Sonnet for the Annunciation', 9 April 2018 <https://malcolmguite.wordpress.com/2018/04/09/a-sonnet-for-the-annunciation-7/>, 9 April 2018, viewed 27 August 2018.

Epilogue

[1]   Job 38:2 and 4.

[2]   Printed by kind permission of my friend, Nicky Brown.

[3]   de Chardin, Teilhard, *The Heart of Matter* (London: Collins, 1978), p. 26.

Copyright acknowledgements